IF YOU WANT TO WRITE

Brenda Ueland

GENERAL PRESS

Published by
GENERAL PRESS
4805/24, Fourth Floor, Krishna House
Ansari Road, Daryaganj, New Delhi - 110002
Ph : 011-23282971, 45795759
E-mail : generalpressindia@gmail.com

www.generalpress.in

First Edition : 2020

ISBN : 9789389716290

Published by Azeem Ahmad Khan for General Press

BESTSELLING FICTION

- 1984 by George Orwell
  Fiction/Classics, ISBN: 9789380914947
- A Tear and a Smile by Kahlil Gibran
  Fiction/Classics, ISBN: 9788180320477
- Alice's Adventures in Wonderland by Lewis Carroll
  Children's/Classics, ISBN: 9789380914046
- Animal Farm by George Orwell
  Fiction/Classics, ISBN: 9789380914701
- Black Beauty by Anna Sewell
  Children's/Classics, ISBN: 9788180320095
- Demian by Hermann Hesse
  Fiction/Classics, ISBN: 9789387669567
- Gitanjali by Rabindranath Tagore
  Fiction/Poetry, ISBN: 9789380914886
- Selected Stories of Nietzsche by Friedrich Nietsche
  Fiction/Short Stories, ISBN: 9788180320491
- Siddhartha by Hermann Hesse
  Fiction/Classics, ISBN: 9789380914145
- Tales from India by Rudyard Kipling
  Fiction/Short Stories, ISBN: 9789380914411
- The Hound of the Baskervilles by Sir Arthur Conan Doyle
  Fiction/Classics, ISBN: 9789380914534
- The Light of Asia by Sir Edwin Arnold
  Religion/Buddhism, ISBN: 9789380914923

Search the book by its ISBN

Contents

1. Everybody is Talented, Original and has Something Important to Say. 7

2. Imagination is the Divine Body in Every Man. 13

3. Why a Renaissance Nobleman Wrote Sonnets. 18

4. The Imagination Works Slowly and Quietly 26

5. Sooner Strangle an Infant in Its Cradle than Nurse Unacted Desires. 35

6. Know that There is Often Hidden in us a Dormant Poet Always Young and Alive. 43

7. Be Careless, Reckless! Be a Lion! Be a Pirate! When You Write 54

8. Why you are not to be Discouraged? Annihilated by Rejection Slips 61

9. People Confuse the Human and the Divine Ego 71

10. Why Women who do too much Housework should Neglect it for Their Writing 78

11. Microscopic Truthfulness 89

12. Art is Infection 98

13. The Third Dimension 105

14. Keep a Slovenly, Headlong, Impulsive, Honest Diary . . .114

15. You do not Know What is in You—an Inexhaustible Fountain of Ideas 125

16. On Using the Imagination .138

17. The Tigers of Wrath are Wiser than the Horses of Instruction 144

18. He whose Face Gives No Light shall Never Become a Star 151

1

Everybody is Talented, Original and has Something Important to Say

I have been writing a long time and have learned some things, not only from my own long hard work, but from a writing class I had for three years. In this class were all kinds of people: prosperous and poor, stenographers, housewives, salesmen, cultivated people and little servant girls who had never been to high school, timid people and bold ones, slow and quick ones.

This is what I learned: that everybody is talented, original and has something important to say.

And it may comfort you to know that the only people you might suspect of *not* having talent are those who write very easily and glibly, and without inhibition or pain, skipping gaily through a novel in a week or so. These are the only ones who did not seem to improve much, to go forward. You cannot get much out of them. They give up working presently and drop out. But these, too, were talented underneath. I am sure of that. It is just that they did not break through the shell of easy glibness to what is true and alive underneath,—just as most people must break through a shell of timidity and strain.

Everybody is Talented

Everybody is talented because everybody who is human has something to express. Try *not* expressing anything for twenty-four hours and see what happens. You will nearly burst. You will want to write a long letter or draw a picture or sing, or make a dress or a garden. Religious men used to go into the wilderness and impose silence on themselves, but it was so that they would talk to God and nobody else. But they expressed something: that is to say they had thoughts welling up in them and the thoughts went out to someone, whether silently or aloud.

Writing or painting is putting these thoughts on paper. Music is singing them. That is all there is to it.

Everybody is Original

Everybody is Original, if he tells the truth, if he speaks from himself. But it must be from his *true* self and not from the self he thinks he *should* be. Jennings at Johns Hopkins, who knows more about heredity and the genes and chromosomes than any man in the world, says that no individual is exactly like any other individual, that no two identical persons have ever existed. Consequently, if you speak or write from *yourself* you cannot help being original.

So remember these two things: you are talented and you are original. Be sure of that. I say this because self-trust is one of the very most important things in writing and I will tell why later.

This creative power and imagination is in everyone and so is the need to express it, i.e., to share it with others. But what happens to it?

It is very tender and sensitive, and it is usually drummed out of people early in life by criticism (so-called "helpful criticism" is often the worst kind), by teasing, jeering, rules, prissy teachers, critics, and all those unloving people who forget that the letter killeth and the spirit giveth life. Sometimes I think of life as a process where everybody is discouraging and taking everybody else down a peg or two.

You know how all children have this creative power. You have all seen things like this: the little girls in our family used to give play after play. They wrote the plays themselves (they were very good plays too, interesting, exciting and funny). They acted in them. They made the costumes themselves, beautiful, effective and historically accurate, contriving them in the most ingenious way out of attic junk and their mothers' best dresses. They constructed the stage and theater by carrying chairs, moving the piano, carpentering. They printed the tickets and sold them. They made their own advertising. They drummed up the audience, throwing out a drag-net for all the hired girls, dogs, babies, mothers, neighbors within a radius of a mile or so. For what reward? A few pins and pennies.

Yet these small ten-year-olds were working with feverish energy and endurance. (A production took about two days.) If they had worked that hard for school it probably would have killed them. They were working for nothing but fun, for that glorious inner excitement. It was the creative power working in them. It was hard, hard work but there was no pleasure or excitement like it and it was something never forgotten.

But this joyful, imaginative, impassioned energy dies out of us very young. Why? Because we do not see that it is great and important. Because we let dry obligation take its place. Because we don't respect it in ourselves and keep it alive by using it. And because we don't keep it alive in others by *listening* to them.

For when you come to think of it, the only way to love a person is not, as the stereotyped Christian notion is, to coddle them and bring them soup when they are sick, but by listening to them and seeing and believing in the god, in the poet, in them. For by doing this, you keep the god and the poet alive and make it flourish.

How does the creative impulse die in us? The English teacher who wrote fiercely on the margin of your theme in blue pencil: "Trite, rewrite," helped to kill it. Critics kill it, your family. Families are great murderers of the creative impulse, particularly husbands. Older brothers sneer at younger brothers and kill it. There is that American pastime known as "kidding,"—with the result that everyone is ashamed and hang-dog about showing the slightest enthusiasm or passion or sincere feeling about anything. But I will tell more about that later.

You have noticed how teachers, critics, parents and other know-it-ails, when they see you have written something, become at once long-nosed and finicking and go through it gingerly sniff-ing out the flaws. AHA! a misspelled word! as though Shakespeare could spell! As though spelling, grammar and what you learn in a book about rhetoric has anything to do with freedom and the imagination!

A friend of mine spoke of books that are dedicated like this: "To my wife, by whose helpful criticism..." and so on. He said the dedication should really read: "To my wife. If it had not been for her continual criticism and persistent nagging doubt as to my ability, this book would have appeared in *Harper's* instead of *The Hardware Age*."

So often I come upon articles written by critics of the very highest brow, and by other prominent writers, deploring the attempts of ordinary people to write. The critics rap us savagely on the head with their thimbles, for our nerve. No one but a virtu-oso should be allowed to do it. The prominent writers sell funny articles about all the utterly crazy, fatuous, amateurish people who *think* they can write.

Well, that is all right. But this is one of the results: that all people who try to write (and all people long to, which is natural and right) become anxious, timid, contracted, become perfectionists, so terribly afraid that they may put something down that is not as good as Shakespeare.

And so no wonder you don't write and put it off month after month, decade after decade. For when you write, if it is to be any good at all, you must feel free,—free and not anxious. The only good teachers for you are those friends who love you, who think you are interesting, or very important, or wonderfully funny; whose attitude is:

"Tell me more. Tell me all you can. I want to understand more about everything you feel and know and all the changes inside and out of you. Let more come out."

And if you have no such friend,—and you want to write,—well then you must imagine one.

Yes, I hate orthodox criticism. I don't mean great criticism, like that of Matthew Arnold and others, but the usual small niggling, fussy-mussy criticism, which thinks it can improve people by telling them where they are wrong, and results only in putting them in straitjackets of hesitancy and self-consciousness, and weazening all vision and bravery.

I hate it not so much on my own account, for I have learned at last not to let it balk me. But I hate it because of the potentially shining, gentle, gifted people of all ages, that it snuffs out every year. It is a murderer of talent. And because the most modest and sensitive people are the most talented, having the most imagination and sympathy, these are the very first ones to get killed off. It is the brutal egotists that survive.

Of course, in fairness, I must remind you of this: that we writers are the most lily-livered of all craftsmen. We expect more, for the most peewee efforts, than any other people.

A gifted young woman writes a poem. It is rejected. She does not write another perhaps for two years, perhaps all her life. Think of the patience and love that a tap-dancer or vaudeville acrobat puts into his work. Think of how many times Kreisler has practiced trills. If you will write as many words as Kreisler has practiced trills I prophesy that you will win the Nobel Prize in ten years.

But here is an important thing: you must practice not perfunctorily, but with all your intelligence and love, as Kreisler does. A great musician once told me that one should never play a single note without hearing it, feeling that it is true, thinking it beautiful.

And so now you will begin to work at your writing. Remember these things. Work with all your intelligence and love. Work freely and rollickingly as though they were talking to a friend who loves you. Mentally (at least three or four times a day) thumb your nose at all know-it-alls, jeerers, critics, doubters.

And so that you will work long hours and not neglect it, I will now prove that it is important for *yourself* that you do so.

2

Imagination is the Divine Body in Every Man

William Blake

I have proved that you are all original and talented and need to let it out of yourselves; that is to say, you have the creative impulse.

But the ardor for it is inhibited and dried up by many things; as I said, by criticism, self-doubt, duty, nervous fear which expresses itself in merely external action like running up and downstairs and scratching items off lists and thinking you are being efficient; by anxiety about making a living, by fear of not excelling.

Now this creative power I think is the Holy Ghost. My theology may not be very accurate but that is how I think of it. I know that William Blake called this creative power the Imagination and he said it was God. He, if anyone, ought to know, for he was one of the greatest poets and artists that ever lived.

Now Blake thought that this creative power should be kept alive in all people for all of their lives. And so do I. Why? Because it is life itself. It is the Spirit. In fact it is the only important thing about us. The rest of us is legs and stomach, materialistic cravings and fears.

How could we keep it alive? By using it, by letting it out, by giving some time to it. But if we are women we think it is more important to wipe noses and carry doilies than to write or to play the piano. And men spend their lives adding and subtracting and dictating letters when they secretly long to write sonnets and play the violin and burst into tears at the sunset.

They do not know, as Blake did, that this is a fearful sin against themselves. They would be much greater now, more full of light and power, if they had really written the sonnets and played the fiddle and wept over the sunset, as they wanted to.

I have to stop here and tell you a little about Blake. This is to show you the blessings of using your creative power. To show you what it is (which may take me a whole book) and what it feels like.

Blake used to say, when his energies were diverted from his drawing or writing, "that he was being devoured by jackals and hyenas." And his love of Art (i.e., expressing in painting or writing the ideas that came to his Imagination) was so great that he would see nothing but Art in anything he loved. And so, as he loved the Apostles and Jesus, he used to say that "they were all artists."

God he often called the "Poetic Genius" and he said "He who loves feels love descend into him and if he has wisdom, may perceive it is from the Poetic Genius, which is the Lord."

Now this free abundant use of his creative power made him one of the happiest men who ever lived. He wrote copious endless poetry (without the slightest hope or concern that it would ever be published). For a time he thought that if he wrote less he would do more engraving and painting. He stopped it for a month or more. But he found on comparison that he did more painting when he let out this inspired visionary writing. All of which proves, I think, that the more you use this joyful creative power—like the little girls producing the plays—the more you have.

As for Blake's happiness—a man who knew him said: "If asked whether I ever knew among the intellectual, a happy man, Blake would be the only one who would immediately occur to me."

And yet this creative power in Blake did not come from ambition. (I think ambition injures it and makes it a nervous strain and hard work.) He burned most of his own work. Because he said: "I should be sorry if I had any earthly fame, for whatever natural glory a man has is so much detracted from his spiritual glory. I wish to do nothing for profit. I wish to live for art. I want nothing whatever. I am quite happy."

As an old man, his wish for a little girl was "that God might make His world as beautiful to her as it had been to him."

He did not mind death in the least. He said that to him it was just like going into another room. On the day of his death he composed songs to his Maker and sang them for his wife to hear. Just before he died his countenance became fair, his eyes brightened and he burst into singing of the things he saw in heaven.

"The death of a saint!" said a poor charwoman who had come in to help Mrs. Blake.

Yet this was the man who said most of us mix up God and Satan. He said that what most people think is God is merely prudence, and the restrainer and inhibitor of energy, which results in fear and passivity and "imaginative dearth."

And what we so often call "reason" and think is so fine, is not intelligence or understanding at all, but just this: it is arguing from our *memory* and the sensations of our body and from the warnings of other people, that if we do such and such a thing we will be uncomfortable. "It won't pay." "People will think it is silly." "No one else does it." "It is immoral."

But the only way you can grow in understanding and discover whether a thing is good or bad, Blake says, is to do it. "Sooner strangle an infant in its cradle than nurse unacted desires."

For this "Reason" as Blake calls it (which is really just caution) continually nips and punctures and shrivels the imagination and the ardor and the freedom and the passionate enthusiasm welling up in us. It is Satan, Blake said. It is the only enemy of God. "For nothing is pleasing to God except the invention of beautiful and exalted things." And when a prominent citizen of his time, a logical, opining, erudite, measured, rationalistic Know-it-all, warned people against "mere enthusiasm," Blake wrote furiously (he was a tender-hearted, violent and fierce red-haired man): "Mere Enthusiasm is the All in All!"

I tell you all this because I hope to prove to you the importance of your working at writing[1] at some creative thing that you care about. Because only if I can make you feel *that,* will you do it and persist in it. And not only for the next few weeks! I want you to do it for years to come, all your life!

We have come to think that duty should come first. I disagree. Duty should be a by-product. *Writing,* the creative effort, the use of the imagination, should come first,-at least for some part of every day of your life. It is a wonderful blessing if you will use it. You will become happier, more enlightened, alive, impassioned, lighthearted and generous to everybody else. Even your health will improve. Colds will disappear and all the other ailments of discouragement and boredom.

I know a very great woman who makes her living by teaching violin lessons in the daytime. (Her name is Francesca and I may have to speak of her later.) Then from midnight until five o'clock in the morning, she is happy because she can work on her book. This is her daily routine. The book is her life work. She has been

---

1. Whenever I say "writing" in this book I also mean anything that you love and want to do or to make. It may be a six-act tragedy in blank verse, it may be dress-making o r acrobatics, o r inventing a new system of double entry book-keeping. But you must be *sure* that your imagination and love are behind it, that you are not working just from grim resolution, i.e., to make money or impress people.

working at it for thirty years. In it she hopes to explain to people how they can learn to play the violin beautifully in two years instead of ten, and she wants them to know this, because playing great music will do so much for them (all).

One day she came to me and had a very bad cold. "Oh, lie down quick!" I exclaimed, "and I will get you some hot lemonade and put a shawl over yourself."

She opened her eyes wide at me, and said almost with horror in her voice.

"Oh, *that* is no way to treat a cold!... No, I slumped a little yesterday and so I caught it. But I worked all night and it is much, much better now."

Now, you see, I have established a reason for your working at writing, not in a trifling, weak way, but with affection and endurance. In other words, I want to make you feel that there is a great intrinsic reward to writing. Unless you feel that you will soon give it up. You won't last very long at it. A few rejection slips will flatten you out. A few years of not making a cent out of it will make you give it up and feel bitterly that it was a waste of time.

I want to assure you with all earnestness, that no writing is a waste of time,—no creative work where the feelings, the imagination, the intelligence must work. With every sentence you write, you have learned something. It has done you good. It has stretched your understanding. I know that. Even if I knew for certain that I would never have anything published again, and would never make another cent from it, I would still keep on writing.

3

Why a Renaissance Nobleman Wrote Sonnets

Now perhaps the thoughts, "There is no money in it," and "It may never be published," you find dry up all the springs of energy in you, so that you can't drag yourself to a piece of paper.

I have experienced this often. I have cleared it up for myself in this way:

At the time of the Renaissance, all gentlemen wrote sonnets. They did not think of getting them in the *Woman's Home Companion*. Well, why write a sonnet at all then?

Now one reason is (and this is very fine and commendable) the hope of getting it in the *Woman's Home Companion*. But there are many other reasons more important. And incidentally unless you have these other reasons, the sonnet won't have much vitality and the *Woman's Home Companion* will send you a rejection slip.

A Renaissance nobleman wrote a love sonnet for a number of reasons. A slight and very incidental reason may have been that he wanted to show people he could do it. But the main reason was to tell a certain lady that he loved her: (although they also wrote beautiful sonnets then about all sorts of things: sonnets that were prayers, that were indignant business letters, that were political arguments).

But say the nobleman wrote a sonnet to tell the lady that he loved her. His chest was full of an uncomfortable pent-up feeling that he had to express. He did it as eloquently, beautifully and passionately as he could, on paper.

And although his sonnet was never published in any magazine, and he never got a cent for it, he was not unrewarded any more than a person who sings a beautiful Bach choral is unrewarded and needs to be paid for it—any more than the little ten-year-old girls who produced the plays had to have fifty cents an hour and the regular union rates.

One of the intrinsic rewards for writing the sonnet was that then the nobleman knew and understood his own feeling better, and he knew more about what love was, what part of his feelings were bogus (literary) and what real, and what a beautiful thing the Italian or the English language was.

If you read the letters of the painter Van Gogh you will see what his creative impulse was. It was just this: he loved something—the sky, say. He loved human beings. He wanted to show human beings how beautiful the sky was. So he painted it for them. And that was all there was to it.

When Van Gogh was a young man in his early twenties, he was in London studying to be a clergyman. He had no thought of being an artist at all. He sat in his cheap little room writing a letter to his younger brother in Holland, whom he loved very much. He looked out his window at a watery twilight, a thin lamppost, a star, and he said in his letter something like this: "It is so beautiful I must show you how it looks." And then on his cheap ruled note paper, he made the most beautiful, tender, little drawing of it.

When I read this letter of Van Gogh's it comforted me very much and seemed to throw clear light on the whole road of Art.

Before, I had thought that to produce a work of painting or literature, you scowled and thought long and ponderously and weighed everything solemnly and learned everything that all artists had ever done aforetime, and what their influences and schools were, and you were extremely careful about *design* and *balance* and getting *interesting planes* into your painting, and avoided, with the most stringent severity, showing the faintest *academical* tendency, and were strictly modern. And so on and so on.

But the moment I read Van Gogh's letter I knew what art was, and the creative impulse. It is a feeling of love[2] and enthusiasm for something, and in a direct, simple, passionate and true way, you try to show this beauty in things to others, by drawing it.

The difference between Van Gogh and you and me is, that while we may look at the sky and think it is beautiful, we don't go so far as to show someone else how it looks. One reason may be that we do not care enough about the sky or for other people. But most often I think it is because we have been discouraged into thinking what we feel about the sky is not important.

And Van Gogh's little drawing on the cheap note paper was a work of art because he loved the sky and the frail lamppost against it so seriously that he made the drawing with the most exquisite conscientiousness and care. He made it as much like what he loved as he could. You and I might have made the drawing and scratched it off roughly. Well, that would have been a good thing to do too. But Van Gogh made the drawing with seriousness and truth.

This is what Van Gogh wrote about people like all of us, whose creative impulse is confused (and not simple as his was) and mixed up with all sorts of things such as the wish to make an impression (not just to tell the truth) and to do what critics say artists should do, and so on.

---

2. Or it can be a feeling of hate and abhorrence too. Though the work of the men who have worked from Jove seems to be greater than those who have worked from hate.

He said:

"When I see young painters compose and draw from *memory*,[3] and then haphazardly smear on whatever they like *also from memory*,—then keep it at a distance and put on a very mysterious, gloomy face to find out what in Heaven's name it may look like, and at last and finally make something from it, always from *memory*,—it sometimes disgusts me, and makes me think it all very tedious and dull.

"They cannot understand that the figure of a laborer,—some furrows in a plowed field, a bit of sand, sea and sky,—are serious objects, so difficult but at the same time so beautiful, that it is indeed worth-while to devote one's life to the task of expressing the poetry hidden in them."

To show that the creative impulse of Van Gogh, a great genius, was simply loving what he saw and then wanting to share it with others, not for the purpose of showing off, but out of generosity, I will tell you a few things he said. I want to show you that what he had in him is just what you all have in yourselves and should let out. For I must remind you again and again that that is the whole purpose of this book.

Van Gogh said:

"My only anxiety is what I can do... could I not be of use and good for something?... And in a picture I wish to say something that would console as music does."

He said:

"We take beautiful walks together. It is very beautiful here, if one only has an open and simple eye without any beams in it. But if one has that it is beautiful everywhere."

He said:

"Painters understand nature and love her and teach us to see her."

And this:

---

3. The italics are his.

"When we drove back from Zundert that evening across the heath, father and I got out and walked awhile; the sun was setting red behind the pine trees, and the evening sky was reflected in the pools; the heath and the yellow and white and gray sand were so full of harmony and sentiment,—see, there are moments in life when everything within us too is full of peace and sentiment, and our whole life seems to be a path through the heath, but it is not so always."

And this:

"What has changed is that my life was then less difficult, but as to the inward state that has not changed. If there has been any change at all, it is that I think and believe and love more seriously now what I already thought and believed and loved then."

This:

"Oh, while I was ill there was a fall of damp and melting snow, I got up at night to look at the country. Never, never had nature seemed to me so touching and so full of feeling."

And this:

"In a few years I must finish a certain work. I need not hurry myself; there is no good in that—but I must work on in full calmness and serenity, as regularly and concentratedly as possible, as briefly and concisely as possible.

"The world only concerns me in so far as I feel a certain debt and duty towards it and out of gratitude[4] want to leave some souvenir in the shape of drawings or pictures,—not made to please a certain *tendency in art*, but to express sincere human feeling."

You can see how Van Gogh's simple impulse is in all of us. But in us it is clouded over and confused with notions such as:

---

4. The italics are mine. And you see he worked from love and generosity. Yet the world treated Van Gogh about as badly as it could treat anyone. As the result of poverty and starvation he went insane and died. A pseudo artist who worked for fame to *impress* the world, would have felt very much aggrieved indeed.

will the work be good or bad? or would it be Art? or would it be modernistic enough and not academical? and would it sell? would it be economically sound to put the time in trying to do it?

Well, Van Gogh was one of the great painters. During his life he made only 109 dollars in all on his paintings. They are now worth about two million dollars. He had a terribly hard life—loneliness, poverty and starvation that led to insanity. And yet it was one of the greatest lives that was ever lived—the happiest, the most burningly incandescent. And see, a few words he has written in his letters, these many years after his death, have changed my whole life!

And one of the most important of these intrinsic rewards is the stretched understanding, the illumination. By painting the sky, Van Gogh was really able to see it and adore it better than if he had just looked at it. In the same way (as I would tell my class), you will never know what your husband looks like unless you try to draw him, and you will never understand him unless you try to write his story.

I tell you these things because of my own difficulties. One great inhibition and obstacle to me was the thought: will it make money? But you find that if you are thinking of that all the time, either you don't make money because the work is so empty, dry, calculated, and without life in it. Or you *do* make money and you are ashamed of your work. Your published writings give you the pip.

Another great stumbling block and inhibition to me was the idea that writing (since I wanted to make a fortune and dazzle the public)[5] was something in which you showed off, were a virtuoso, set yourself up to be something remarkable.

---

5. Remember though that any motive that makes you feel like writing is fine. Use it. Start. If you want to dazzle the public, try it. Good luck to you. In my case it was an inhibition and resulted in nauseous work and I just want to explain that after a while the public-dazzling motive may give out and your results disappoint you.

But at last I understood from William Blake and Van Gogh and other great men, and from myself—from the truth that is in me (and which I have at last learned to declare and stand up for, as I am trying to persuade you to stand up for *your* inner truth)—at last I understood that writing was this: an impulse to share with other people a feeling or truth that I myself had. Not to preach to them, but to give it to them if they cared to hear it. If they did not—fine. They did not need to listen. That was all right too. And I would never fall into those two extremes (both lies) of saying: "I have nothing to say and am of no importance and have no gift"; or "The public doesn't want good stuff."

When I learned all this then I could write freely and jovially and not feel contracted and guilty about being such a conceited ass; and not feel driven to work by grim resolution, by jaw-grinding ambition to *succeed*, like some of those success-driven business men who, in their concern with action and egoistic striving, forget all about love and the imagination, and become sooner or later emotionally arthritic and spiritually as calcified and uncreative as mummies.[6] (I understand these things because I have experienced them, though on a small scale. I try not to rail against what I have not experienced myself.)

Yes, it has made me like working to see that writing is not a performance but a generosity.

But if egotism and exhibitionism started you working I am grateful. It was the greatest of blessings. For by working you will pass through it and tap a greater and more exuberant motive.

6. They will be uncreative in business as well as in everything else. For of course the creative power is expressed in business as well as in other things. I know a business man whose every sentence has more life, creative vision and generosity in it than those of many artists.

But the trouble with business expressing the creative power freely and prodigally as Art does, you cannot be recklessly generous in business, giving higher and higher wages and all your products freely and lovingly to the public.

I find that I wrote this to someone three years ago:

"Forgive me, but perhaps you should write again. I think there is something necessary and life-giving about 'creative work' (forgive the term).[7] A state of excitement. And it is like a faucet: nothing comes unless you turn it on, and the more you turn it on, the more comes.

"It is our nasty twentieth century materialism that makes us feel: what is the use of writing, painting, etc., unless one has an audience or gets cash for it? Socrates and the men of the Renaissance did so much because the rewards were intrinsic, i.e., the enlargement of the soul.

"Yes we are all thoroughly materialistic about such things. 'What's the use?' we say, of doing anything unless you make money or get applause? for when a man is dead he is dead.' Socrates and the Greeks decided that a man's life should be devoted to 'the tendance of the Soul' (Soul included intelligence, imagination, spirit, understanding, personality) for the soul lived eternally, in all probability.

"I think it is all right to work for money, to work to have things enjoyed by people, even very limited ones; but the mistake is to feel that the work, the effort, the search is not the important and the exciting thing. One cannot strive to write a cheap, popular story without learning more about cheapness. But enough. I may very well be getting to raving."

And so now I have established reasons why you should work from now on until you die, with real love and imagination and intelligence, at your writing or whatever work it is that you care about. If you do that, out of the mountains that you write some mole hills will be published. Or you may make a fortune and win the Nobel Prize. But if *nothing* is ever published at all and you never make a cent, just the same it will be good that you have worked.

---

7. To say the word "creative" has always embarrassed me. So many unctuous people have over-used it. But I have to use it. It is what I mean.

4

The Imagination Works Slowly and Quietly

Now I am going to try to tell you what the creative power is, how you can detect it in yourself and separate it out from all your nervous doubts and checks. And how you can separate it from mere memory. For memory and erudition (i.e., the superimposed lumber of all the hard facts you have learned) can smother it very easily.

When we hear the word "inspiration" we imagine something that comes like a bolt of lightning, and at once with a rapt flashing of the eyes, tossed hair and feverish excitement, a poet or artist begins furiously to paint or write. At least I used to think sadly that that was what inspiration must be, and never experienced a thing that was one bit like it.

But this isn't so. Inspiration comes very slowly and quietly. Say that you want to write. Well, not much will come to you the first day. Perhaps nothing at all. You will sit before your typewriter or paper and look out of the window and begin to brush your hair absentmindedly for an hour or two. Never mind. That is all right. That is as it should be,—though you must sit before your typewriter just the same and know, in this dreamy time, that you are going to write, to tell something on paper, sooner or later. And you also must know that you are going to sit here tomorrow for a while, and the next day and so on, forever and ever.

Our idea that we must always be energetic and active is all wrong. Bernard Shaw says that it is not true that Napoleon was always snapping out decisions to a dozen secretaries and aides-de-camp, as we are told, but that he moodled around for months. Of course he did. And that is why these smart, energetic, do-it-now, pushing people so often say: "I am not creative." They are, but they should be idle, limp and alone for much of the time, as lazy as men fishing on a levee, and quietly looking and thinking, not *willing* all the time. This quiet looking and thinking is the imagination; it is letting in ideas. Willing[8] is doing something you know already, something you have been told by somebody else; there is no new imaginative understanding in it. And presently your soul gets frightfully sterile and dry because you are so quick, snappy and efficient about doing one thing after another that you have not time for your own ideas to come in and develop and gently shine.

When you will, make a resolution, set your jaw, you are expressing an imaginative fear that you *won't* do the thing. If you knew you would do the thing, you would smile happily and set about it. And this fear (since the imagination is always creative) comes about presently and you slide down into the complete slump of several weeks or years—the very thing you dreaded and set your jaws against.

And why do these grim-resolution people will? Because they are full of fear which drives them to try to dominate themselves and others for the purpose of making money or getting some kind of security. If you dominate and boss your children all the time, it means you are afraid *they* will not be secure, foolishly thinking that your bossing will guarantee this, that you know just

8. No doubt my terms would horrify a psychologist but I do not care at all.

how they should grow. Or by willing you try to dominate yourself so that your importance, financial or artistic or ethical or whatever, will be secure.

But the great artists like Michelangelo and Blake and Tolstoy—like Christ whom Blake called an artist because he had one of the most creative imaginations that ever was on earth—do not want security, egoistic or materialistic. Why, it never occurs to them. "Be not anxious for the morrow," and "which of you being anxious can add one cubit to his stature?"

So they dare to be idle, i.e., not to be pressed and duty-driven all the time. They dare to love people even when they are very bad, and they dare not to try and dominate others to show them what they must do for their own good. For great and creative men know what is best for every man is his own freedom so that his imagination (it can also be called the conscience or the Holy Ghost) can grow in its own way, even if that way, to you or to me, or to policemen or churchgoers, seems very bad indeed.

But since I would not be a critic for anything, i.e., tell you where you are all wrong without telling you something that might make you feel like changing, know that I will do so. I will try to show the grim-resolution people how they might become imaginative, creative ones.

It is these fool, will-worshiping people who live by maxims and lists of chores and the Ten Commandments—not creatively as when a fine, great maxim occurs to you and bursts a little, silent bomb of revelation in you—but mechanically.

"... Honor thy father and thy mother"... the active, willing, do-it-now man thinks and makes note of this daily, sets his jaw, and thinks he does honor them, which he does not at all, and which of course his father and mother know and can feel, since nothing is hidden by outer behavior.

The idle creative man says:

"'Honor thy father and mother.'... That is interesting... I don't seem to honor them very much... I wonder why that is?" and his imagination creatively wanders on until perhaps it leads him to some truth such as the fact that his father is a peevish and limited man, his mother unfortunately rattle-brained. This distresses him and he puzzles and thinks and hopes again and again for more light on the subject and tries everything his imagination shows to him, such as being kinder or controlling his temper; and perhaps he comes to think: "Is it *they* who are peevish and boring, or is it just that I, being a small man, think so?" And he goes on and seeks and asks for the answer with his imagination. And who knows, in time he even may come to understand what Christ did (who as I said was one of the most imaginative men who ever lived and whose life was fiercely and passionately directed against following mechanically any rules whatever): how if one is great and imaginative enough one can honor and love people with all their limitations.

So you see the imagination needs moodling,—long, inefficient, happy idling, dawdling and puttering. These people who are always briskly doing something and as busy as waltzing mice, they have little, sharp, staccato ideas, such as: "I see where I can make an annual cut of $3.47 in my meat budget." But they have no slow, big ideas. And the fewer consoling, noble, shining, free, jovial, magnanimous ideas that come, the more nervously and desperately they rush and run from office to office and up and downstairs, thinking by action at last to make life have some warmth and meaning.

The great mystic philosopher Plotinus said about this:

"So there are men too feeble for contemplation." (This is his word for what I call the imagination.) "Being unable to raise themselves to contemplation from the weakness of their Soul, unable to behold spiritual reality and fill themselves with it, but desiring to see it, they are driven to action that they may see that which they could not see with the spiritual eye."

But I must go back to my subject,—writing.

If you write, good ideas must come welling up into you so that you have something to write. If good ideas do not come at once, or for a long time, do not be troubled at all. Wait for them. Put down the little ideas however insignificant they are. But do not feel, any more, guilty about idleness and solitude.

But of course I must say this:

If your idleness is a complete slump, that is, indecision, fretting, worry, or due to over-feeding and physical mugginess, that is bad, terrible and utterly sterile. Or if it is that idleness which so many people substitute for creative idleness, such as gently feeding into their minds all sorts of printed bilge like detective stories and newspapers, that is too bad and utterly uncreative.[9]

But if it is the dreamy idleness that children[10] have, an idleness when you walk alone for a long, long time, or take a long, dreamy time at dressing, or lie in bed at night and thoughts come and go, or dig in a garden, or drive a car for many hours alone, or play the piano, or sew, or paint *alone*; or an idleness—and this is what I want you to do—where you sit with pencil and paper or before a

---

9. I personally include much of the shouting, broken, perfunctory talk of social life, most card playing, and all reading that passes over a person without affecting him in the least. I mean reading that just passes time. But of course that affects him,—slowly rotting his soul.

10. You will say that children are not alone for hours every day, or they do not want to be, and they are creative. But children are not willing all the time. They have lifted off them all duty, all anxiety. When a child is taken somewhere by his parents he is not thinking nervously: are they late or early? Is the furnace running at home? etc., but he is at rest and looks out the window and sees and thinks. He lives in the present. That is why children enjoy looking and listening so much. Why they are such wonderful mimics of grown-ups. They have tremendous concentration because they have no other concern than to be interested in things. Later they are trained to force concentration and become as imaginatively muddy and uneasy as the rest of us.

typewriter quietly putting down what you happen to be thinking, that is creative idleness. With all my heart I tell you and reassure you: at such times you are being slowly filled and re-charged with warm imagination, with wonderful, living thoughts.

Now some people when they sit down to write and nothing special comes, no good ideas, are so frightened that they drink a lot of strong coffee to hurry them up, or smoke packages of cigarettes, or take drugs or get drunk. They do not know that good ideas come slowly, and that the more clear, tranquil and unstimulated you are, the slower the ideas come but the better they are.

It was Tolstoy who showed me this. I used to drink coffee all day and smoke two packages of cigarettes. I could thus pump myself up to write all day and much of the night, for a few days. But the sad part of it was, what I wrote was not very good. It came out easily, but it wasn't much good. It was interlarded with what was pretentious, commonplace and untrue.[11]

This is what Tolstoy said about it:

"'If I do not smoke I cannot write. I cannot get on. I begin and I cannot endure,' is what is usually said and what I used to say. What does it really mean?

"It means either that you have nothing to write, or what you wished to write has not yet matured in your consciousness, but it is only beginning dimly to present itself to you, and the appraising critic within[12] when not stupefied with tobacco, tells you so.

---

11. I tell in another chapter why things that are so, are uninteresting. Though I filled a whole British Museum with such stuff, not only would nobody care to read it, but it would do me no good to write it.

    If I wrote something true and good that nobody cared to read, it would do me a great deal of good.

12. By "critic" he means here what I call the true self, the imagination, or the Holy Ghost, or the Conscience. It is what is always searching in us and trying to free what we *really* think, from what we think we ought to think, from what is super-imposed by bossy parents, teachers or literary critics.

"If you did not smoke, you would either abandon what you have begun, or you would wait until your thought has cleared itself dimly in your mind; you would try to penetrate into what presents itself dimly to you,"—(by, as I say, idling, by a long, solitary walk, by being alone)—"would consider the objects that offer themselves and would turn all your attention to the elucidation of the thought. But you smoke and the critic within you" (the truth-seeking creative critic) "is stupefied, and the hindrance to your work is removed. What to you, when not inebriated by tobacco, seems insignificant, again seems important; what seemed obscure, no longer seems so; the objections that present themselves vanish and you continue to write and write much and rapidly."

I am not urging you not to smoke. Each must find out all things for himself. But I want to show how Tolstoy knew good thoughts come slowly. And so it is nothing for you to worry about or to be afraid of, and it is even a bad plan to hurry them artificially.

For when you do so, there may be suddenly *many* thoughts, but that does not mean that they are specially good ones or interesting. It is just as when you give a thoughtful, slightly tired person a stiff drink. Before the drink he says nothing but what seems to him interesting and important. He mentally discards the thoughts that are not important enough to make up for the fatigue of saying them. But after the drink, all his thoughts come out head over heels, whatever crosses his mind. There are suddenly *many* thoughts; but they are just like the flutter of thoughts that come out of one of those unfortunate people who cannot keep from

---

This critic in us all, I love. The critic I abhor is the one (inside or out) which is always measuring, comparing, cautioning and advising prudence and warning against mistakes and quoting authorities and throwing dry, anxious doubts into everyone, by showing them just the way they must go.

No, each man must go by his own Conscience, by his own creative, truth-searching critic.

talking all the time. This kind of talking is not creation. It is just mental evacuation.

And it is Tolstoy who showed me the importance of being idle,—because thoughts come so slowly. For what we write today slipped into our souls some *other* day when we were alone and doing nothing.

Tolstoy speaks of the hero of Dostoevsky's "Crime and Punishment."

"Raskolnikof lived his true life, not when he murdered the old woman or her sister. When murdering the old woman herself, and especially when murdering her sister, he did not live his true life, but acted like a machine doing what he could not help doing—discharging the cartridge with which he had long been loaded. Raskolnikof lived his true life... at the time when he was lying on the sofa in his room . . . . And then—in that region quite independent of animal activities—the question whether he would or would not kill the old woman was decided. That question was decided when he was doing nothing and only thinking; when only his consciousness was active and in that consciousness tiny, tiny alterations were taking place. It is at such times that one needs the greatest clearness to decide correctly the questions that have arisen, and it is just then that one glass of beer, or one cigarette, may prevent the solution of the question, may postpone the decision, stifle the voice of conscience, prompt the decision of the question in favor of one's lower animal nature, as was the case of Raskolnikof."

I tell you this not to persuade you to give up drinking and smoking (though that might be a good thing too) but to show you that what you write today is the result of some span of idling yesterday, some fairly long period of protection from talking and busyness.

It was Raskolnikof lying on the couch, ill and miserable and in despair about his destitute mother and sister, and wondering what to do,—it was then he created the murder that came many days later.

In the same way what you write today you thought and created in some idle time on another day. It is on another day that your ideas and visions are slowly built up, so that when you take your pencil there is something to say[13] that is not just superficial and automatic, like children yelling at a birthday party, but it is true and has been tested inwardly and is based on something.

And why it must be true I will explain later. I do not mean it must be a statement of fact such as "Columbus discovered America in 1492," but it must come from your true self and not your theoretical self, from what you really think, love and believe, not from your hope to make an impression.

That is why I hope you can keep up this continuity and sit for some time every day (if only for a half hour, though two hours is better and five is remarkable and eight is bliss and transfiguration!) before your typewriter,—if not writing then just thoughtfully pulling your hair. If you skip for a day or two, it is hard to get started again. In a queer way you are afraid of it.[14] It takes again an hour or two of vacant moodling, when nothing at all comes out on paper; and this is difficult always because it makes us busy, efficient Anglo-Saxons with our accomplishment-mania, feel uneasy and guilty.

You see I am so afraid that you will decide that you are stupid and untalented. Or that you will put off working as so many wonderfully gifted people do, until that time when your husband can retire on full pay and all your children are out of college.

---

13. Though remember this: you may not be conscious, when you sit down, of having evolved something important to say. You will sit down as mentally blank, good natured and smiling as usual, and not frowning solemnly over the weight of your message. Just the same, when you begin to write, presently something will come out, something true and interesting.

14. I hope to explain why you are afraid of it before this book is finished and to show you why you need not be at all.

5

Sooner Strangle an Infant in Its Cradle than Nurse Unacted Desires

William Blake

I do not mean to inveigh against action. Action is glorious and we have to act. "Unacted desires breed pestilence," said Blake.

That is why you must not just moodle forever[15] Some people act (i.e., express what they have thought of in their idle times) by becoming better people, better doctors, better business men, better mothers.

But in this book I am trying to get you to express it with pencil in hand and put it down and get it out on paper or a canvas, where you can look at it and then if you do not think it is good, continue to

15. If we don't act at all (express our imaginings either in work or a changing personality, so that we can learn and think again something better) we certainly rot.

act by asking God and his angels for a light on it, and then act again. Think and then let it out, act. Always. Think quietly for a time. Express it quietly later; not by will so much as by a kind of faith.

That is why I hope I have not said in this book anywhere "You *must* let it out... You *must* write." There is too much pressure of duty and fear on you already, on everybody,—too many "musts" for the talent in you to begin to shine in a free and jolly way.

I don't warn you against action. I just want to cheer you up by saying that nervous, empty, continually *willing* action is sterile[16] and the faster you run and accomplish a lot of useless things, the more you are dead.

So if you want to write try this: go into your room alone. Resign yourself tranquilly to doing something slow and worthless for at least an hour. Take a pencil or sit before your typewriter and look out of the window. Perhaps write down and name (if you feel like it) what colors you see in the sky—exactly—and absorbedly, with quiet, dreamy attention. "Star... four points... yellow." Don't bother to make sentences (unless you want to). Or dreamily and carelessly write what goes through your head such as: "I don't seem to feel at all like working today. What is this muggy feeling?" (You may find yourself giving a brilliant, truthful, luminous description of dullness and apathy). Or idly scrawl:

"I seem to wish I could write a story that would sell for eight hundred dollars about a duchess but I never knew a duchess and can't seem to see one in my mind's eye and what should I name her anyway?" Thoughts will begin to come out of this. You will find you have something to say. And tomorrow there will be more.

---

16. What people call "will" means you do a thing doggedly or defiantly, while you are allowing your imagination to say that everybody thinks you are no good at it, and it is a fool thing to do anyway.

 People by "will" do remarkable things. But this is for soldiers and money-grubbers who are committed to all sorts of evil that their imagination and Jove tells them is horrible and senseless.

But before I get down to brass tacks and talking about writing itself, I want to say a few more things about the imagination, the creative power in you, and how to detect it and how it works.

I will tell you what I have learned myself. For me, a long five or six mile walk helps. And one must go alone and every day. I have done this for many years. It is at these times I seem to get re-charged. If I do not walk one day, I seem to have on the next what Van Gogh calls "the meagerness." "The meagerness," he said, "or what is called depression." After a day or two of not walking, when I try to write I feel a little dull and irresolute. For a long time I thought that the dullness was just due to the asphyxiation of an indoor, sedentary life (which all people who do not move around a great deal in the open air suffer from, though they do not know it).

But I have come to learn otherwise. For when I walk grimly and calisthenically,[17] just to get exercise and get it over with, to get my walk out of the way, then I find I have not been re-charged with imagination. For the following day when I try to write there is more of the meagerness than if I had not walked at all.

But if when I walk I look at the sky or the lake or the tiny, infinitesimally delicate, bare, young trees, or where-ever I want to look, and my neck and jaw are loose and I feel happy and say to myself with my imagination, "I am free," and "There is nothing to hurry about," I find then that thoughts begin to come to me in their quiet way.

---

17. I have been a fearful self-disciplinarian all my life. But I have learned a thousand-times better way. I would not tell you anything I have not learned myself. But if you find self-control and self-discipline is a better way for *you* than imagination, good. Then you must do it.

And if I ever say "you should" or "you must" or "you ought" in this book it is a survival of my old impulse to boss myself. People who try to boss themselves always want (however kindly) to boss other people. They always think *they* know best and are so stern and resolute about it they are not very open to new and better ideas.

My explanation of it is that when I walk in a carefree way,[18] without straining to get to my destination, then I am living *in the present.* And it is only then that the creative power flourishes.

Of course all through your day, however busy you are, these little times come. But they are very short in most lives. We are always doing something,—talking, reading, listening to the radio, planning what next. The mind is kept naggingly busy on some easy, unimportant, external thing all day.

That is why most people are so afraid of being alone. For after a few minutes of unpleasant mental vacancy, the creative thoughts begin to come. And these thoughts at first are bound to be depressing, because the first thing they say is: what a senseless thing life is with nothing but talk, meals, reading, uninteresting work and listening to the radio.[19] But that is the beginning. It is just where your imagination is leading you to see how life can be better.

---

18. It is hard to be carefree when you have many anxieties. But the more you have, the more necessary it is to feel carefree for a time, so that you will get some new ideas on how to deal with your anxieties.

19. Most talking is merely narrative, memory, which is not creative imagination, as Blake showed me. In conversation you tell something done or thought or said yesterday. It is living in the past, not the present.

    But when talk is truly interesting, then one is living in the present. A change is taking place in the conversers. One tells the other something that he needs or longs to hear, or that frightens him. That is, it effects a change in him.

    I think that is why married people who bore each other conversationally, quarrel. When their feelings are being hurt, there are threats of separation, etc., then they are really being affected, moved, changed. They are living creatively *in the present.* At last their conversation is actually interesting to them. They have the delicious feeling that they are being listened to at last;—not politely but with a strong alternating current and chemical changes taking place in their souls.

    And that is why just reading where only the memory is involved,—to pass time or accumulate facts,—is no good. I don't care if you have accumulated enough facts for three Ph.D.'s.

But if you would only persist. If you would continue to be alone for a long time, amblingly swinging your legs for many miles and living in the present, then you will be rewarded: thoughts, good ideas, plots for novels, longings, decisions, revelations will come to you. I can absolutely prove that.

And I found this. In the days when I thought a walk was just exercise, the ideas did not come until the end. "It is only in walks that are a little too long, that one has any new ideas," I find that I wrote in my diary. I now understand this. It was because I was nearly home and so gave up the willing, the striving to get this calisthenic chore, the walk, out of the way.

At once I felt released, lazy and free. I suddenly lived in the present and not in my destination[20] where I would be (dully enough) reading the newspaper or eating dinner. Suddenly I was seeing how pretty the winter evening was, how black the trees in the phosphorescent moonlight, how the stars are different colors, how egotism is fear and self-preservation, but how there is an egotism that is great and divine. In other words ideas came and even poetic feelings.

And how do these creative thoughts come? They come in a slow way. It is the little bomb of revelation bursting inside you. I found I never took a long, solitary walk without some of these silent, little inward bombs bursting quietly: "I see. I understand that now!" and a feeling of happiness.

You may find that the little bombs quietly burst in you when you are doing other things,—sewing, or carpentering, or whittling, or playing golf, or dreamily washing dishes.

I have found that playing the piano is a wonderful thing for it. Not just "lullabying yourself," as a Russian pianist I know calls it, when you play the same old pieces in the same old way, just agreeably to pass the time, as you eat candy. And don't play the piano

---

20. The foolishness of all this living in the future! like working very hard at something dull all your life so you can retire on plenty of money at eighty.

by grinding at it (people mix up "working" and "grinding" and I hope to show the difference between them), but by working, that is thinking, feeling, hearing, understanding more and more.

Work on a Mozart sonata, say. There is the beautiful sound which suddenly makes the most ordinary things—pieces of furniture, the rain, full of beauty and something touching as though a light had fallen on them. There is the wonderful athletic pleasure of motion in the hands and shoulders. There is the rhythm which is like an inward dancing. And all the time there is the solitude, the hour or two of isolation from daily life so much of which is nervous, cacophonous, where one's attention is unhappily jerked from this to that, so that the imagination inside cannot accumulate its strength and light.

And now I want to try and show you the difference between grinding and working.[21]

Sometimes when I walk I learn a poem, a Shakespeare sonnet, say, as I go along. I have discovered this: if you say a line over and over again, as children do in memorizing, half mechanically, after a long time the nerves and muscles in your brain and jaws will know how to do it automatically.

But all that automatic grinding takes a long, long time. To learn it more easily[22] I do this: I say a line slowly, slowly, slowly, and I can see in my imagination each word and how it looks in print and in reality. If the word is "winds" I see winds. And in my imagination I trace and marvel at the wonderful economy of Shakespeare's grammar.

---

21. These two are confused. That is why, unfortunately, the word "working" is a depressant to happy, exuberant people who usually have ten times the energy of grinds and would love working if they understood it properly.

22. And creatively, that is, so that I understand and have some feeling for poetry and what the poet was trying to say, and so it is added unto me and affects my life thenceforth.

And during these moments of contemplation, of imagination,—in that fraction of a second when my mind seems to open up and take something in forever, I find I walk less and less fast. I slow up. The more I am contemplating (i.e., thinking creatively so that the understanding is stretched) the slower I go and often I stop walking altogether for that moment—that creative instant of getting it, adding it unto myself forever.

I tell you this so that you will stop thinking of the creative power as nervous and effortful; in fact it can be frightened away by nervous straining.

So never bother to grind. Just try to understand something for the time. If you don't, go on to the next. For if you understand the second or third thing, you will suddenly understand the first.

And when you understand a thing, don't grind over and over it, to grind it into your memory, as children play scales on the piano, or students cram for examinations. The moment you understand it, know that it is a part of you forever. The grinding and the repetition is all lost time (due to fear that you won't remember it) which you should be using for newer and greater things.

It is like this: there are wonderfully gifted people who write a little piece and then write it over and over again to make it perfect,—absolutely, flawlessly perfect, a gem. But these people only emit about a pearl a year, or in five years. And that is because of the grind, the polishing,[23] i.e., the fear that the little literary pearl will not be perfect and unassailable. But this is all a loss of time and a pity. For in them there is a fountain of exuberant life and poetry and literature and imagination, but it cannot get out because they are so anxiously busy polishing the gem.

And this is the point: if they kept writing new things freely and generously and with careless truth, then they would know how to fix up the pearl and make it good, in two seconds, with no work at all.

23. This is not justifiable polishing, i.e., to get nearer and nearer to what is true.

Well, I tell you all these things to show you that working is not grinding but a wonderful thing to do; that creative power is in all of you if you give it just a little time; if you believe in it a little bit and watch it come quietly into you; if you do not keep it out by always hurrying and feeling guilty in those times when you should be lazy and happy. Or if you do not keep the creative power away by telling yourself that worst of lies—that you haven't any.

6

Know that There is Often Hidden in us a Dormant Poet Always Young and Alive

De Musset

I used to have to drive myself to work. You cannot imagine what an uncomfortable, effortful thing it was to be supposed to be a writer. To work at all I had to be a jump ahead of the spears—to need money very badly. After three hours of work[24] I would be pithed and exhausted. I could not work in the afternoon or evening at all, because I was absolutely certain I would not be bright then. All fear and conceit.

It was my class who showed me that I was working in the wrong way. For these humble and inexperienced amateurs suddenly—if

24. Except when finishing a story or article. I could work all day then because it was mostly just copying. But to work for an hour or two on the first draft, the first invention, that would nearly kill me. What flying from it! what boredom! what drinks of water! Telephoning and other evasion!

only I could lift fear off them—revealed all of them such wonderful gift.

I learned from them that inspiration does not come like a bolt, nor is it kinetic, energetic striving, but it comes into us slowly and quietly and all the time, though we must regularly and every day give it a little chance to start flowing, prime it with a little solitude and idleness. I learned that you should feel when writing, not like Lord Byron on a mountain top, but like a child stringing beads in kindergarten,—happy, absorbed and quietly putting one bead on after another.

Once I posed for a lot of twelve-year-old girls who wanted to try some oil painting. I said that I would sit for them for three days and all day long, until their portraits of me were all entirely finished and the very best that they could do.

None of these children had painted with oil paints before. I sat in a chair against the sitting room wall with the light from several eastern windows on me, and this battery of four little girls and three adults faced me, peering at me athwart their canvases. I had nothing to do but to watch them for long hours.

Now a roomful of seven adults means always a good deal of noise and loud talking. With four children among them it is din, pandemonium. And children, as we all know, do not have (in school or church or at a lecture) much power of prolonged, silent, focused concentration, especially on something that takes intense mental struggle and effort. And everyone knows what a mysteriously difficult thing it is to draw something if you are not used to it: the weird difficulty of expressing the third dimension on flat paper! to draw a nose front view is just a frightful problem! Moreover, to paint with oil paints for the first time—I can only describe it by saying it is like trying to make something exquisitely accurate and microscopically clear out of mud pies with boxing gloves on.

Well, that is what these children were trying to do. Yet while they were painting me there was utter dead silence in the room.

You could hear their breathing. Only those burning eyes were looking up at me and down again. Perhaps after twenty minutes or so there would be a groan or a yell of despair: "Oh, Brenda! I have made you look so HAG-GY!"

After long periods they would remember that I was merely human and let me rest for a few minutes, but only with reluctance because it was hard to be torn from their work. But the moment their brief rest time came, the deep religious, blissful silence, absorption and contemplation was supplanted by the uproar, shouting, interrupting, whacking and thumping that one normally gets from a roomful of children. Even the dogs who had been peacefully dozing began weaving in and out, barking and wrestling.

Now these children worked for five or six hours at a stretch (and this will be the way you are going to work at your writing) for two and a half days—working with the blissful, radiant power of a Michelangelo or Blake. Their paintings were all remarkable,[25]—all different, astonishing in their own way, because the creative impulse was working innocently, not egotistically or to please someone, an instructor, say, who threw in the anxious questions: is it art? has it balance? design? and so on. The creative power was working innocently, each child simply trying to show in paint what she saw and felt.

I tell you all this because it is the way you are to feel when you are writing—happy, truthful and free, with that wonderful contented absorption of a child stringing beads in kindergarten.

---

25. The colors were very beautiful. A fine portrait painter who saw them cried out, groaned almost, with envy at the colors and the draftsmanship, at the genius that would lead a child to make the floor a pale turquoise instead of its own color, etc.

    Each portrait was entirely different. But each was a portrait of me and my personality (infinitely more so than a photograph), and each was a portrait of the child who painted it and *her* personality. This always happens in writing or painting: what you are, you show.

With complete self-trust. Because you are a human being all you have to do is to get out truthfully what is in you and it will be interesting, it will be good. Salable? I don't know. But that is not the thing to think of—for a long time anyway.

And again I tell you this because I want to show you that the creative impulse is quiet, quiet. It sees, it feels, it quietly hears; and *now*, in the *present*. You see how these children painting my portrait were living in the present? It is when you are really living in the present that you are living spiritually, with the imagination.

I have noticed that two or three very rare, extraordinary, creative people I know, when they are truly magnetic, fascinating, oracular, seem to be living in the present. Francesca is one of them; a little Swedish mystic who sees visions as Blake did is another; and Carl Sandburg, the poet, is the third.

Francesca, for example, *always* seems to be living in the present: now! now![26] You can never get her to gossip chattily, to repeat long narratives or listen to them, not because she disapproves of gossip, far from it, but because to her, I think, mere narrative is not a thing to bother about because it is only memory[27] a recounting of the past in which nothing new can come in. It is not inspiration, the present.

No, she never says very much but sits looking at you with loving, shining eyes, gently swaying as though to unheard music, and listens to you and understands perfectly, and wisdom seems to descend into her gently from some place, from beyond some place,

---

26. Sometimes say softly to yourself: "*Now*... now. What is happening to me now? This is *now*. What is coming into me now? this moment?"

    Then suddenly you begin to see the world as you had not seen it before, to hear people's voices and not only what they are saying but what they are trying to say and you sense the whole truth about them. And you sense existence, not piecemeal—not this object and that—, but as a translucent whole.

27. She tells, of course, things she remembers, but they always throw some light on her present creative moment.

as though she heard and understood in that moment St. Joan's voices. And then she says something (without beginning[28]) that at once seems to me so remarkable, true and important and fills me with something that is wonderfully consoling and illuminating.

I have never heard her talk merely from memory (that is merely repeating something she heard or thought yesterday[29]) but always creatively. She has never uttered a perfunctory word, never anything that was not felt and felt at that very instant.

Carl Sandburg—the poet—I have seen him do this. He talks in his beautiful voice dreamily and inspiration seems to come out of him now... now as he goes along, as though whatever imagination entered into him, out it came freely and like music.

Once driving around the lake by our house we stopped and looked at the sunset, a December sky. He spoke of "the gunmetal sky" and looked for a long time. I felt some awe: "This is really the way a poet feels when he is moved." For I could feel what was going on in him while he looked at the sky,—some kind of an experience, incandescent and in motion. But *I* was living ten minutes hence in the future, feeling a little self-conscious and anxious to please and full of small compunctions, though I exclaimed: "Isn't it perfectly wonderful!" Well, Carl Sandburg was living in the present and having a poetic experience. But I was too full of other cerebrations,

---

28. She always plunges right into the middle of a truth, never leading up to it with apologetic explanations, proofs and qualifying phrases. And that is what I want you to do when you write. And like Francesca, since she is always truthful, never care if you are believed or not.

29. She does not do this consciously at all. She does not plan or *will* to be a person who never repeats things (and God forbid that you should do that!). She is just one of those happy creative people who do not ever waste time accumulating facts and proofs from memory. She just accepts what her imagination shows her and lets out this new truth, without comparing anxiously this and that and testing all for its soundness. I have no doubt she tests truths inwardly. But she does not have to (egotistically) establish her soundness, before people.

concern about being a polite hostess and getting home on time to dinner.

Now you and I and everybody often live in the present before a sunset. And we have felt things about it, just as Carl Sandburg has, or Dante or Shakespeare. Saint-Beuve said: "There exists in most men a poet who died young, whom the man survived." And de Musset said: "Know that there is often hidden in us a dormant poet, always young and alive."

You all know this is so. And since all are poets I suggest living in the present part of the time, as great poets and artists do. Incidentally, when you say perfunctorily about the sky just to talk: "What a beautiful evening!" that is not poetry. But if you say it and mean it very much, it is.

I do not know whether to keep these foregoing passages in this book or not. You might get to scowling and intellectualizing about this and making rules (which you must never, never do!) and saying to yourself: "Be careful. Am I doing this correctly? Is this Memory or Imagination I am using now?"

Heaven forbid that that should happen. Before the end of the book I will probably strike this out so there will be no danger of that. Of *course* we use memory all the time, and the clearer and more copious it is the better. If you are writing stories, of *course* you use your memory and put in all the details of your elopement and so on. But do not forget to keep re-charging yourself as children do, with new thinking called "Inspiration." I just describe this "living in the present" because you might like to try it: that is, be free and open to all things and don't pretend and don't fret.[30]

---

30. Yes, I am all against anxiety, worry. There are many people, you can see, who consider worry a kind of duty. Back of this I think it is the subconscious feeling that Fate or God is mean or resentful or tetchy and that if we do not worry enough we will certainly catch it from Him.

But they should remember that Christ said that we should cast off anxiety so that we could "seek first the Kingdom of Heaven and His righteousness" (i.e.,

See how the Mexicans and southwestern Indians live in the present, doing what they must do happily and quietly and taking no anxious thought for the morrow. They say a Mexican will sit on his haunches smoking a cigarette and happily looking at nothing for hours.

And see how all people in Mexico are such remarkable artists! The poorest Mexican cannot touch any work without making it lovely,—a two-cent tin pail or sandals made out of automobile tires. I think this is because they live in the present. There is more contemplation there: that is to say, they take time to love beauty.

But we northerners have become too much driven by the idea that in *twenty years* we will live, not now: because by that time our savings and the accrued interest will make it possible. To live *now* would be idleness. And because of our fear we have come to think of all idleness as hoggish, not as creative and radiant.

Perhaps I can describe "living in the present" in this way. In music, in playing the piano, sometimes you are playing *at* a thing and sometimes you are playing *in* it.[31] When you are playing at it you crescendo and diminish, following all the signs. "Now it is time to get louder," you read on the score. And so you make it louder and louder. "Look out! Here is a pianissimo!" So you dutifully do that. But this is intellectual and external.

Only when you are playing in a thing do people listen and hear you and are moved. It is because you are moved, because a queer and wonderful experience has taken place and the music—Mozart or Bach or whatever it is—suddenly is yourself, *your* voice and your eloquence. The passionate and wonderful questions in the music are *your* questions. And with all the nobility and violence

---

live creatively, greatly, seekingly, in the present) "and all these things" (beauty, happiness, goodness, talent, food and clothing) "will be added unto you." Of course He is right.

31. I know a fine concert pianist who says sadly of a terribly hardworking but hopeless pupil: "She always practices and never plays."

and wonderful sweetness of Beethoven, say, it is *you* talking to those who listen.

One more example.

Look at those people who have a genius for being funny. When they are mimicking someone you can see that they are really in a kind of trance. They are the person they are mimicking. If instead they are self-conscious (like me) and cannot get lost in this trance, this identification, if they are saying to themselves, "Now I do this and now I go cross-eyed and everybody will laugh," it is not funny at all and everybody looking on is pained and embarrassed and does not know where to look.[32]

Well, this same kind of identification, freedom, carelessness, should be there when you are writing. Then it will be good.

Now some will interpret this as meaning they should stop thinking. No, I don't mean that. When you are writing you will probably think harder than you ever have in your life and more clearly. But self-consciousness, anxiety, "intellectualizing" (i.e., primly frowning through your pince-nez and trying to do things according to prescribed rule as laid down by *others*)[33] will be untied from you, will be cast off.

Dean Inge says that the great mystic philosopher Plotinus described this "living in the present" like this:

"In our best and most effective moments, when we really 'enter into' our work, we leave it behind... This is the experience of Pure Spirit when it is turned toward the One. When we reach

32. Self-consciousness comes from an anxiety that you will *not* impress people. The would-be clown cannot be funny because he is afraid that his audience will not think he is.

The really funny man doesn't think about the audience at all. If it doesn't laugh, he has had his own fun and doesn't care. If the audience laughs it just frees him even more and fills him (Inspiration) with further and more absurd, unpremeditated antics.

33. And bearing in mind a thousand things *not* to do.

this stage we often doubt that the experience is real because the 'senses protest that they have seen nothing.' Hence there is a kind of unconsciousness in the highest experiences of the Soul, though we cannot doubt them, not in the least."

In other words, it is when you are really living in the present—working, thinking, lost, absorbed in something you care about very much, that you are living spiritually.

And so once again I have driven home the point: it will be good for you if you will work at your writing.

One more thing about our feeling that unless we are in action we are either idle or stupid:

You sit down to write, to think (vaguely conceiving of "thinking" as something that a college professor does). No logical thought comes in the first minute or two that you try it. A sort of paralysis follows, a conviction of your mental limitations, and you disconsolately go downstairs to do something menial and easy like washing the dishes, while doing so (though not knowing it) having some wonderful, fascinating, extraordinary, original, illuminating thoughts. Not knowing that they are thoughts at all, or "thinking," you have no respect for them and do not put them down on paper—*which you are to do from now on!* That is, you are always to act and express what goes through you.

And that is the tragedy of so-called worthless people. They perhaps have more thoughts than us rushers, but they never get them out on paper or canvas or in music or work because of many things that I have enumerated: self-doubt, fear of failure, and so on.

The tragedy of bold, forthright, industrious people is that they act so continuously without much thinking, that it becomes dry and empty.[34]

---

34. Very forceful, active men might say that acting makes them *think* better. But if they took more time for idling and thinking, perhaps, the Imagination would show them much greater actions than the ones they are engaged in.

But we have to act. But often the idle man does not act, not because he is lazy but because he is afraid in some way. He does not know that action should follow thought simply and pleasurably with absorption (like the child stringing beads). He thinks action is painful and hopelessly hard[35] and almost certain to end in failure.

Listen to what the poor, great, impassioned Van Gogh said about this:

"Because there are two kinds of idleness," he wrote to his brother, "that form a great contrast. There is the man who is idle from laziness, and from lack of character, from the baseness of his nature. You may if you like take me for such a one...

"Then there is the other idle man, who is idle in spite of himself, who is inwardly consumed by a great longing for action, who does nothing because he seems to be imprisoned in some cage, because he does not possess what he needs to make him productive, because the fatality of circumstances brings him to that point, such a man does not always know what he could do, but he feels by instinct: yet I am good for something, my life has an aim after all, I know that I might be quite a different man! How can I then be useful, of what service can I be! There is something inside me, what can it be!

"This is quite a different kind of idle man; you may if you like take me for such a one. A caged bird in spring knows quite well that he might serve some end; he feels quite well that there is something for him to do, but he cannot do it. What is it? He does not

---

35. Because of all the disciplinarians and Stoics and duty-people in the world. And I do not mean that we should do nothing that is hard and unpleasant. Columbus discovering America went through a hard and uncomfortable time. But it was love and Imagination that got him to do it. He would never have done it from duty alone. Duty would have made him stay sternly at home making money and rearing his children in the way they should go. No, he would never have attempted anything so rash, free and glorious from duty!

remember quite well. Then he has some vague ideas and says to himself: 'The others make their nests and lay their eggs and bring up their little ones,' and then he knocks his head against the bars of the cage. But the cage stands there and the bird is maddened by anguish.

"'Look at the lazy animal,' says another bird that passes by, 'he seems to be living at his ease.' Yes, the prisoner lives, his health is good, he is more or less gay when the sun shines. But then comes the season of migration. Attacks of melancholia,—'but he has got everything he wants,' say the children that tend him in his cage. He looks at the overcast sky and he inwardly rebels against his fate. 'I am caged, I am caged, and you tell me I do not want anything, fools! You think I have everything I need. Oh, I beseech you, liberty, to be a bird like other birds!'

"A certain idle man resembles this bird... A just or unjustly ruined reputation, poverty, fatal circumstances, adversity, that is what makes men prisoners... Do you know what frees one from this captivity? It is very deep, serious affection. Being friends, being brothers, love, that is what opens the prison by supreme power, by some magic force. But without this one remains in prison.

"There is where sympathy is renewed, life is restored.

"And the prison is also called prejudice, misunderstanding, fatal ignorance of one thing or another, distrust, false shame... But I should be very glad if it were possible for you to see in me something else than an idle man of the worst type."

7

Be Careless, Reckless! Be a Lion! Be a Pirate! When You Write

Now I want to tell some things I have learned about writing from my class.

Though everybody is talented and original, often it does not break through for a long time. People are too scared, too self-conscious, too proud, too shy. They have been taught too many things about construction, plot, unity, mass and coherence.

My little brother wrote a composition when he was twelve and almost every third sentence was: "But alas, to no avail!" That is the sort of thing that everybody does for many years. That is because they have been taught that writing is something special and not just talking on paper.

Another trouble with writers in the first twenty years, is an anxiety to be effective, to impress people. They write pretentiously. It is so hard not to do this. That was my trouble.

For many years it puzzled me why so many things I wrote were pretentious, lying, high-sounding, and in consequence utterly dull and uninteresting. It was a regular horror to read them again. Of course they did not sell either, not one of them.

The explanation of this I learned from my class. Again and again after a few weeks of a kind of rollicking encouragement, they would all—even those whose work seemed hopelessly dull, trite, angular and commonplace—they would break through this, as from a cocoon, and write suddenly in a living, true, touching, remarkable way. It would happen suddenly, overnight. They would break through from composition-writing, theme-writing, to some freedom and honesty and to writing with what I call "microscopic truthfulness."

What made them do this? I think I know. I think I helped them to do it. And I did not do it by criticism, i.e., by pointing out all the mediocrities in their efforts (and so making them contract and try nervously to avoid all sorts of faults). I helped them by trying to make them feel freer and bolder. Let her go! Be careless, reckless! Be a lion, be a pirate! Write any old way.

Francesca helped me to understand this. When giving violin lessons she never tells a child that he is playing a bad note.[36] Why do that? He knows it himself. All are trying to get nearer and nearer to the true pitch, to perfection, anyway. Why fix their attention on the avoidance of mistakes? It just tightens them up, contracts them, and makes them dislike lessons. Moreover, when they are thinking so vividly about the bad notes that they are warned to avoid, they play them again and again, just as a man learning to ride a bicycle goes into the tree he is afraid of. To play a note *truly*, as the simplest person knows, your mind must be on the true note, your Imagination hearing it as you *want* to play it.

---

36. Francesca also told me that all people have an ear for music and can sing in pitch. Some think they cannot, but that is only because they have not learned to hear rightly; and some cannot because they are too tense and try too hard.

I found that many gifted people are so afraid of writing a poor story that they cannot summon the nerve to write a single sentence for months. The thing to say to such people is: "See how *bad* a story you can write. See how dull you can be. Go ahead. That would be fun and interesting. I will give you ten dollars if you can write something thoroughly dull from beginning to end!" And of course no one can.

Try this yourself. It is a relief and you see then how you are not dull at all. It is just as guilty people who are always trying to be so good, should try to be very bad and resolve to stick to it. They would find then how natural it comes to them to be good and would not strain after it, which makes them hypocrites, though in a nice way.

Well, when I told the timid people in the class to see how badly they could write it would give them the courage to venture a few little sentences. And since everybody who is human cannot say a sentence without revealing something—something mild or violent or waggish in their souls—or without having something fine in it, I would point this out. Courage would expand and they would gradually write more.

To show you how people's writing expands under encouragement I will tell you of some of my pupils. And what happened to these few, happened to all of them, except, as I said, to those to whom writing is an easy, glib, superficial babbling. For these are apt to give it up soon, before they break through the shell of glibness to what is true underneath.

Sarah McShane (I will call her) is Irish and unmarried and perhaps thirty. She is plainly and humbly dressed and because of her pallor and wide cheekbones and slanting eyes, she looks Chinese in a very beautiful way. She is so shy though that she cannot look at you directly. But when she talks she cannot keep her sad face immobile but has to smile widely and reluctantly every now and then, from both humor and bashfulness. She is a stenographer and works for nine hours a day in the sub-basement of a department store.

The first writing she showed me was a fat, little note-book about an inch and a half thick. It was filled with neat typing. "Four Days in Glacier Park" by Sarah McShane, 1935.

The first sentence was:

> "There's always something fascinating about a passing freight train—the big, black engine with the ugly, bony arm on its side, the string of box-cars with sometimes a munificent supply of tramps sitting on the top, the heavy oil tanks, and bringing up in the rear, the stove-piped caboose. One and all, from youth to old age, will stand and watch it in silence and with interest."

Well, as soon as I read: "the big, black engine with the ugly, bony arm on its side,"I knew that she could write. She could see and describe things. What she saw and felt, she put down. She did not have the impulse (as those of us who are much better educated) to put down what she felt and then think: "No, it must be fancier than that, like: 'The engine like the charging steed of the prairies.' Or plainer, like: 'The engine with its high wheels.'"

What she felt, what struck[37] her—"the ugly, bony arm on its side"—she put that down. That was a good beginning. I told her what a graphic description these few words were.

As I read along a little I came to this:

> "The new air-conditioned train was a curiosity in itself—no cinders, no smoke, no stifling air—instead an even, cool, clean atmosphere. The interior was painted a delicate green, a bath—or bedroom shade. There were new silver

37. She didn't *try* to be struck. It just quietly happened. Another person would be quietly struck by something else.

> racks for the suitcases, small, delicate, white lights for the night-time, and soft, easy parlor-chair seats for the passengers. A deluxe layout it was indeed."

From this I could see (and tell her) that she had a simple, open eye and noticed everything with quiet pleasure and put it down just as she saw it. And she had a quiet enthusiasm. She liked pretty colors: "delicate green," "silver." And this naïve truthfulness and enthusiasm, love for things, showed that there was a great deal of poetry and creative power in Sarah McShane, and that she was a simple and good person (which also would show in her writing and shine through it) and she chose simple, short and poetic words the way the poets in Ireland do. She was Irish and had a soft and very beautiful voice. That, I saw at once, meant that she could write too.

In the fat notebook she told everything that she noticed: what time trains pulled in and out, the towns passed.

> "Familiar things slid by us as we chugged along from one Twin City to the other. Smokestacks and tanks; houses and trees; gaudy signboards; the big flour mills; the Mississippi River—all rolled by in panoramic review.
>
> "Out at Wayzata,[38] Lake Minnetonka, a cold blue in color, lay stretched to the left, shivering in rolling white caps. Mirrored in its waters was the sun's golden face, haloed in an effect of glittering color."

---

38. This told me much about Sarah McShane. She worked in a subbasement and was glad to see Wayzata! a commonplace little town fourteen miles from home. She felt joy and gratitude. This especially meant she could write. Enthusiasm! this is the sign that the creative fountain is in you. "Enthusiasm is the All in All," said Blake. I must tell you this often.

I like this description very, very much: "shivering in rolling white caps." That was just right, because she told it as she felt it and so I felt it too. "The sun's golden face haloed in an effect of glittering color." I liked that too. I like it now as I write it.

She told of the hotels they stayed in.

> "'How can I stay here,' I thought the minute I stepped inside the door... The rough woodwork gave the room a cold, woodsy, rainy-day touch... Martha was more easily pleased. She plunked herself down m the wicker chair and pulled off her shoes.

From this fine sentence I saw and knew then all about Martha.

> "For dinner that first evening we had fruit compote, chicken okra (soup) with a heaped dish of crackers, grilled sirloin, a little bell-shaped cup with a ball of something in it, mashed potatoes, buttered peas, creamed onions, celery, buns and coffee, and for dessert, butterscotch ice cream and cake."

Yes, she could write because she told everything simply, as it was, and didn't put on airs.

> "After studying the glacier, we spent some time watching the mountain goats on the rocky crags of the peaks. With the human eye we could only faintly make them out—white specks moving around. One lady, the wife of the big man, had a pair of field glasses, and she let us look through them.
>
> "After I had looked through them, for a long time, she asked, 'Did you see the goats?"
>
> "'Yes.' I was merely being polite.

> "But I didn't see the goats. I didn't see anything. All I saw was the blurred, watery surface of the lens. I have never been able to see any more than that through field glasses."

The class burst out laughing when I read this.

"You see you are funny too," I said to Sarah McShane. "See how they are all laughing? You write wonderfully well, and you have humor tool" She reddened with delight.

8

Why you are not to be Discouraged? Annihilated by Rejection Slips

Sarah McShane Finished the account of her trip as the classes went on. I wanted to get her gradually to become freer and more personal. She was like so many gentle and modest people. They mix up the human and the Divine ego.[39] They feel they are not important and hate to say "I." And to hide the "I" modestly and keep it down, they will write long travelogues, say,—"Afoot in the Rockies," giving altitudes, facts, statistics, hotel accommodations, things out of the almanac that everybody knows already or can look up if they care to.

Now to have things alive and interesting it must be personal, it must come from the "I": what *I* know and feel. For that is the only great and interesting thing. That is the only truth you know, that nobody else does. Sarah McShane—! wanted to free her into writing more about herself, to speak from herself and know that she was important.

39. I think I know what the difference is. I will try to tell about that later.

But I never told her this as a schoolmarmish criticism, saying: "You must be more careful to put in more personal details."

She would have dragged them in all right, little undigested, mechanical gobbets such as "I did indeed enjoy the view from Mt. Grinnell!"

No, I didn't do that. Instead I just told her how good it was, how interesting and showed her places that proved it. "Tell more," I said. "Tell everything you can possibly think of. You speak here of this truck-driver whose tight clothes fitted him like the skin of a bulldog. What a bright picture!—Did he really say that? call the woman 'a yellow-headed lion?... How extraordinary!... What makes you think he felt that way about his wife?"

Soon she was writing, covering many, many pages with vivid, clear, lucid writing, describing the life and people around her, her inner life.

I tell of Sarah McShane not because she is more remarkable than the others but because she had almost not a trace of literary sophistication. She had had no courses in Browning and Tennyson, no talk at home about Dickens and Louisa M. Alcott.

> "Arnold Benedict or Benedict Arnold!" she wrote in her diary. "Which one was it? Benedict Arnold, he was the traitor, wasn't he? And that other one, the writer of the diary, that's the one I am trying to get at. Arnold Benedict, or was it Arnold Bennett?"

She goes on to say how Arnold Bennett said he could write 1000 words in go minutes.

"I wonder," she says, "how many words I could write in an hour and a half. It's nine fifteen now." (This, after a nine-hour day in the sub-basement.) She sets about it and writes 700 words.

"But my papers fell on the floor and I had to stop and pick them up, my shoes hurt and I had to pull them off, and I had to stop and find page 275 in 'David Copperfield,' and think for awhile, once or twice. Subtract this from the whole and maybe I could have made it—1000 words in go minutes."

And the point is, not a word of her diary is empty or automatic. Every word is alive and interesting. And to me her diary is just as interesting as much of Arnold Bennett's, and certainly it is much more poetic and full of feeling.

I tell about her because she has so much farther to go in writing than many of the others. (Of course her writing has led her to reading good literature,—Dickens and many others to see how *they* do it-since the only way ever to have an intelligent understanding of anything, and a true interest in it, whether it is writing or art or aviation, is to do it yourself.)

And I tell about Sarah McShane because although she is the least self-assertive person in the world and angelically humble, she has a passionate craving to write. She wrote alone. She searched for help and advice, took a correspondence course that cost a hundred dollars, though she said in her diary, "It was not exactly what I wanted. It was newspaper writing in which the important facts are put first.[40] Too, they always gave assignments. I wanted to write things choosing my own subjects."

40. It has long seemed queer to me that newspaper writing is supposed to be so terse and lively. People take courses in journalism, etc. "Oh, he has had *newspaper* experience,'" we are told of some writer, with solemn respect.

Yet the newspaper formula of mechanically forcing a half dozen dry facts into the first long sentence, and then throughout the column, repeating for four or five times what was said before, is about as dull, difficult and impenetrable as any writing could be.

I know that in most newspapers I never seem to have the consummate will power to get any farther than the headlines.

I tell this because it shows that the longing to write must be in thousands of the most unobtrusive people who have not the least hope of making money or cutting a literary figure.

Well, here are a few of the pages out of her thick notebook:

* * *

Sunday, Dec. 6, 1936

I went to eight o'clock mass this morning. Usually I go to seven. Father Corrigan speaks then and I love his sermons. He speaks so much on the little things of life. He is a big man and although he has but one lung, yet he can be heard anywhere in the church, and doesn't seem to speak loud either. He is never well—never without pain, yet he never complains. All his parishioners love him. What would St. Mark's do without him? Sometimes the things he speaks on are the common faults of the day, and it happens that sometimes I had been guilty of those things during the week. I used to imagine then that he was looking at me, that he knew I did those things. "How did he know I did that?" I would think, and wish for a hole in the seat to sink through.

When I came home mother was lying on the couch.

"You'll have to get your own breakfast," she said, "I'm sick." Mother is getting old and I often tell her not to get my breakfasts, not to bother about me. I can get my own, but she pays no attention. The breakfast is always there, sitting on the table, waiting for me. Mother had a sick headache. She gets them frequently and must stay in bed, sometimes a whole day. When she hasn't the headache, then it's the rheumatism. She is seldom without pain.

After breakfast I was getting ready to wash the dishes and father came out of the dining room door. I can always tell when he's coming. His cane goes tromp, tromp on the floor. Father is

---

This is not the fault of the subject matter, since everything in the world is interesting. but of the writing.

old now. His hair is white, and his face is kind. He has the queer notion that old people should be fat. He often measures himself and if he's not four feet around the waist he begins to worry and eats more. He thinks there's something wrong.

I washed the dishes and he wiped them. I love to do the dishes. I often think that if I were ever to lose my job I'd try and get one washing dishes somewhere. And father likes to do them too. He loves housework anyway. He can cook as good as any woman. Although I never have seen him make a cake or pie, he has many times made bread—and good bread. I believe he would sooner work in the house than do any other kind of work.

After we finished the dishes I prepared to scrub the floor. Mother didn't scrub it yesterday. She wasn't feeling well, and it needed scrubbing badly. It must have been dirty when I noticed it. That's what mother would say, which is quite true.

Just as I began looking for the mop and pail, I heard footsteps in the dining room. It was mother. She was up and moving around. I didn't want her to know I was going to scrub the floor. She would not want me to if she knew it.

So I tiptoed downstairs, into the basement looking for a pail. Pails are scarce in our house. We have only two. I found one, but it had some green water in it, perhaps something new my brother was experimenting with. He's always experimenting with something. I went back twice to throw the green water out, then didn't. The other pail I couldn't find, but over near the washing machine on the floor was an old skillet that had seen its best days...

I had a faint memory of mother using some kind of powder once in scrubbing the floor, so I put some gold dust powder into the skillet and filled it with hot water. Then I commenced scrubbing the floor. Hardly was I started when mother came out the dining-room door.

"Never mind the floor," she said, "I'll scrub it after dinner." It was typical of her. Never wants me to do any of the housework.

Thinks I do enough when I work all day. If I were not working, just staying home, mother wouldn't have to do a thing. She could just do the things she likes—sew, read, crochet, knit, play solitaire, and work jig-saw and crossword puzzles. I have often suggested that we hire someone to come in once a week and wash and clean the house, but no, she will not listen to that. She would feel hurt and think it was because we thought she wasn't doing her work.

I don't know what I'd do without my father and mother. They are the most precious "things" in the world. I often think as I get up in the morning and the house is warm, how much that means. Father gets the fire going around 5:30 and by 6:30 it is warm and snug.

* * *

Well, you see she writes well, so lucidly and simply and without one superfluous word and makes us know the life of herself and her family, just how they all feel and think and exactly how they live. And all through, though she says nothing specifically about how they look, yet you even seem to see them too as though you would know them if you met them in the street. Even the brother who is not there, who makes experiments with green water in a pail—you seem to know all about him too.

* * *

I now look through several of this month's big, shiny magazines in which all the writers are well educated and prominent and get hundreds of dollars for what they write. I find no writing in the stories that is better than Sarah McShane's, or as good, i.e., that draws you through it with such a quiet believing interest.

Here is a paragraph of Faith Baldwin's, one of the most highly paid of all writers.

> Old Man Bradley sat up in bed and shook his head clearing the mist from his eyes. He slid his feet to the floor, shuffled

> them into his carpet slippers, and sat there listening... Early. He'd slip in and warn the boys to be quiet, and then he'd go into the bathroom before the others were. He passed his hand over the stubble of his chin. He could shave now and go downstairs and get things started for Winnie. The decision seemed momentous. As a rule he waited to shave until the children were at school and their mother and father off to work. It would be a luxury to shave before breakfast. At home he had always done so—made you feel a decent, complete man, coming downstairs with your face clean and smooth. You enjoyed your breakfast more.

This is not as good as Sarah McShane's writing. You can see how it is taking this writer more words to tell less; that is, you don't see or know old Mr. Bradley as well as you do Sarah McShane's father. And when the magazine writer says "the decision was momentous," I know that at that point I begin to think: "No, it wasn't momentous, I don't believe it, and so I am now reading just fiction, hocum, and she puts that in to over-persuade me, or to make it sound like writing."

But try this for yourself. Take any block of fiction in any current magazine and it will not be as good, as living or cling in your memory as Sarah McShane's writing does.

I open "Of Mice and Men" because it is not just popular fiction but "stark realism" as the book reviewers say, and "sincere" Art. The writing is different from Sarah McShane's but it is no better, no more convincing or alive. It has more vocabulary. But as a matter of fact my compassion for the people in it does not seem to turn over at all. But it does for Sarah McShane and her family.[41]

Now I know it is not fair to compare fiction with a diary, with the truth. Fiction is much harder to write well, i.e., as though it

---

41. This may be prejudice and because, like everybody, I get so fond of the people I try to help.

were true. So I will turn to the articles in the current magazines wherein people write from the facts, the truth, what they believe and have experienced.

Here is one in the Pictorial Review:

> We mothers of today, with girls just growing into womanhood, do not need to be told that we are facing a difficult world; everyone of us in her heart realizes that she needs all the understanding and wisdom there is in her, if she is to be a help to her children.
>
> It is no use not to recognize the reality of change. There has been a sharper cleavage in thought and conduct between this generation and our own, than there has been for many years, and the difference is not in superficialities but in fundamentals.

Not as good as Sarah McShane's. Long, complex words, not short, poetic ones. Hard to read and needs concentrating. And when your thought has plowed all through it, all through that coagulation of "womanhood... generation... superficialities and fundamentals" you see she is just saying something that you knew already. There is no news in it and it is what hundreds are saying, and on top of that, probably isn't true.

And that first sentence, "We mothers of today, with girls just growing into womanhood, do not need to be told that we are facing a difficult world." Well, why tell it then? Why take up the reader's time with that long, opaque sentence? Sarah McShane would not over-explain that way. She would take you straight to the center. "Many mothers face a problem"—which would be easier to read, more interesting and better writing.[42]

---

42. I do not mean that only *I* say this, but so would Carlyle, Ibsen, Henry James, George Bernard Shaw, Dostoevsky and others.

And here is an article about home life, as Sarah McShane's writing is. It is in *McCall's* and by Mrs. Roosevelt. Mrs. Roosevelt writes, beginning her article, "My Home."

> It is natural, of course, that when I think of my home, I should think first, just now of the White House! I remember well seeing it when Mrs. Hoover showed me through. Surprising as it may seem, I registered in my mind the number of rooms, their positions and how many people I could take care of, but while I perhaps realized that the furniture would have to be changed, as a good deal of it belonged personally to the President and Mrs. Hoover, the details of the furnishings made little impression on me.
>
> When we came in on Inauguration Day and I went up to the second floor with the knowledge that we were really going to live there, I must confess to being a little appalled by that empty feeling which a house devoid of all personal things can give you.

No. Sarah McShane writes better than Mrs. Roosevelt.

Now I am not finding fault with the magazines at all for publishing what they do and not Sarah McShane's work. There are a thousand reasons for it. And it does not matter if Sarah McShane's writing is better than Mrs. Roosevelt's, and Mrs. Roosevelt would be the first to be glad of it. And these magazine writers that I have quoted perhaps a little derisively and meanly have so many things to bemuse them, throw them off the track, so that they cannot discover their clear, true self as Sarah McShane has, and write from that. They must think: "Is this what the editor wants?... Is this discreet?... Does this sound as magazine writing is supposed to sound?"

I tell all this for just this reason: because I want to show you that millions of human beings, with education and without it, think and feel things that are worth saying and then can write them just beautifully, like great men and women and true poets.

I want you all to know that. This is so that you will not be discouraged, annihilated by rejection slips, and too much awed and inhibited by successful writers, but will work along in your own way, as Sarah McShane does.

9

People Confuse the Human and the Divine Ego

There was a woman in our state who lived in the country and wrote very successfully articles for magazines and syndicated paragraphs for the newspapers about small town and country life.

The class talked of her talent and success a little wistfully and some of them copied what she had written reverently, in their diaries.

Here is an excerpt. I will write it here and interpolate why I think it is not as good as it might be.

> "How quiet it seems after the threshing machine vanishes behind the bend in the road. The place seems empty. You wish they could come back, the threshing crew, with their swearing and laughter and quarreling. How sober, the children even, and what long faces. Behind the barn looms up a gleaming, yellow stack of straw—unfamiliar and alarming in appearance" (unfamiliar maybe, but not alarming), "but it is a monument to a husband's toil

and sweat and suddenly it grips you profoundly." (No, it doesn't.) "Life becomes intensely precious." (I cannot feel she means this, because of just looking at the straw stack.)

"Maybe the well-dressed man in fashion forecasts will be wearing light coats and spats and such" (dragged in to be amusing) "but in this part of the country there will be several well-dressed men wearing high-top boots lavishly" (sissy humor, i.e., not felt but for effect) "decorated with mud and barnyard insignia; scarecrow effects will be especially featured" (dragged in to be amusing) "sweaters with frayed sleeves and fringed bottoms, flapping overalls, caps stiff with accumulations of grease, cream and dust." (This is good because it is true and inwardly felt.)

"Unlike Longfellow's immortal pause, that of the country woman, during this season of cornhusking, comes between the dawn and the daylight" (dragged in to be literary) "that nebulous" (I don't think she really means "nebulous") "ten or fifteen minutes during which she has a little time of her own. The kitchen is warm, the breakfast is cooking, the children: are :hot yet up, the husband has not yet come in from the barn, and suddenly there seems to be nothing to do. Can it be true?" (Of course it is true! It happens every morning.) "This moment is one of the sweetest of the whole day: a moment in which she can sit at an east window and watch the daybreak from its pink satin shell." (I like this very much.) "A moment unbelievably beautiful." (But somehow I don't believe this now. I feel this is gushing, i.e., not felt. If it were felt, truly experienced, I would believe it.)

From this you can see that whatever is bogus, put on, isn't good and a bore. At least so it seems to me.

A member of the class wrote this about farm life when she became freed enough just to put down truthfully and carelessly what she remembered about it.

* * *

Perhaps it was just the joy of being snug and warm while the wind thrashed things about outdoors—but I loved the wind itself, and it gave me a kind of peace to hear it.

I rolled my hands round and round the spool-turned posts of the couch with its corn-husk mattress, and sniffed the slightly musty odor contentedly because it was so homey. And traced with my fingers the featherstitching between the patches of the couch cover—that cover pieced of discarded men's suits, browns and grays and dark blue serge, a record of quiet winter afternoons near the stove.

The clock ticked with a kind of little stammer as it stood on its narrow shelf above the newspaper rack; there was an occasional quacking of ducks, and the afternoon freight train raced by with its usual perturbed rhythm.

I turned my eyes to the pictures hung high on the wall neat the molding: a print of Noah's Ark with the animals... entering safely two by two; the current calendar of the General Mercantile Company, with snow on the house tops represented by tinsel glitter; a photograph of the good grandma surrounded by a wreath of wax flowers and framed in walnut.

That made me think of what Pauline had told me a few days before. She said that her mother had promised that when grandpa died, she—Pauline—and all her sisters could go to the funeral. After all, he was not *my* grandpa. Could *I* be included in that adventure too, I wondered. Oh, I hoped so. Not that I wanted grandpa to die, for in spite of his grumpiness, he was kind, and often gave us pin-striped peppermints, and told us about the days in Missouri where he had lived as a boy. It was just that funerals were so beautiful. Pauline and I had had a glimpse of one not long before, in the neighborhood. It had been a drowsy afternoon, and through the open windows of the house we heard the sounds of the parlor organ and of a hymn being sung. The yard was full of horses and wagons, and relatives came from everywhere. We inhaled the fragrance of flowers sent from "the Cities," and watched with lively interest as so many grown people came out crying. "Oh, look at *that* one," we whispered to one another time after time in a kind of melancholy contest as to who should discover the loudest sobber.

So now I sometimes caught myself looking at Grandpa with macabre interest, though a little ashamed of my thoughts. Still, would he mind very much? He was so old. I was rather vague about the matter of age, but imagined he must be almost fifty anyway. Well, we would see. For the present it was enough just to lie there and think of nothing. There was plenty of time for a nap before the afternoon lunch would be set out on the large oilcloth-covered table in the center of the room. There would be milk and coffee and sausage and cheese and jelly and cookies. And today was the day for fresh bread, spread with lots and lots of butter.

...Maybe it would rain a little, it was beginning to look dark. I did not mind, for then we would race from house to summer kitchen with shawls over our heads, and squeal with delight as someone else stepped into the puddles.

The sound of the wind grew louder, and I raised myself on my elbow to look out. Yes, it was blowing hard. A rooster, looking very silly with his feathers all this-way-and-that, scurried across the yard toward the comfort of the coop. A branch from one of the nearby trees struck sharply against the window pane. The old rope swing jerked back and forth with nervous irregularity. Wisps of hay from the mows back of the reaper shed were scattered about the grass.

Beneath the harsher sound of the wind, I heard a low moaning—that was from the row of willows below the garden. And that was what I liked best. I lay back to listen with closed eyes, and felt myself slipping away—deliciously away. The windows rattled but I liked that too. It was all familiar, assuring—and safe. Never was there so satisfying a time or place for the pleasure of sleep—cradled by the wind, and know that at the end of the soothing darkness I should awaken to the sight of friendly faces, and the sound of kindly, well-known voices.[43]

* * *

This writing, you see, is very beautiful. It is impossible to cut it. I try to take out a sentence here or there, but cannot bring myself to do it. They are all too good and necessary and contribute too much. And so it is Art, literature, belles lettres, or whatever you want to call it.

But I am not saying to you: "Look at this. Do like this. This is good, the other is bad." Not at all. I am saying that all people have in them this power to write greatly and well, when they express freely and carelessly what is true to THEM.

If I did not tell you that, if like most teachers and critics I just said: "Now this is really good! Study this!" and praised it to the skies, then you would try to write like it. And then it would not be any good at all. No, write from yourself.[44]

The person who wrote this farm memory so well lived alone, had no family, had lost her job. She was pale, preternaturally diffident, and blocked by the most convinced self-depreciation, and she had a blank, cold, uneasy look on her face and an almost inaudible, indecisive, little voice. She was pretty, though, and wore tiny, stylish hats and had a wonderful, wide-stretched, all-comprehending laugh.

The first night in the class, she timidly, almost inaudibly, said that she sometimes thought she would like to be a newspaper columnist. She timidly showed me a sentence or two:

> "Usually it is depressingly dreary-that view from my window—cinders, parked cars, sagging fence, tired—

43. By Elsa Krauch.

44. I hope to show you how to do this later,—at least to help you.

looking, low buildings. Then one morning—the deep, fresh snow"... And so on.

"You write very, very well," I said. This is not flattery. I said it to her—I have said it too many others. But I always mean it and it is always true.

Now, within two years, she has written a good and successful book. She supports herself by writing, by translations and other work. Her writing will grow freer and better, truer and more abundant all the time. I am sure that she has a fine, important life ahead of her.

For accomplishment, I guess she is my star pupil so far. In so short a time she has lifted herself to this high level of self-confidence. Now she has true self-respect and boldness and will stand up for the intelligence, the light, the gift that is in her, no matter what happens in this life or in the life eternal.

And perhaps I can explain here what I think is the difference between the human ego and the Divine ego. By self-confidence and boldness I do not mean conceit (the human ego). Conceit is very different. It is a static state where you rest on some past (or fancied) accomplishment. Then you rest on your oars and say to all (in so many words): "Look at me. I did that!" But self-confidence never rests, but is always working and striving, and it is always modest and grateful and open[45] to what is new and better. I think that is why boasting is vaguely disagreeable and one always regrets it: "Why did I boast? That is done. Why rest and smack my lips over that? Do something new and better."

But you never regret your sense of power and understanding inside, i.e., the Divine ego. And this should always be increasing.

And you must learn to do this: if you write something and they all tell you it is bad,—editors, critics, everybody,—think it over and you may become convinced that they are right (though

45. And so it is really humble all the time before what is greater than itself.

you are not to be ashamed or discouraged for a minute, but keep on writing).

But if they all tell you it is bad and you still think in your soul that what you wrote was *good*,—if you find that you still believe what you wrote and feel it and it is true to *you*, then you must stand by it. And it might help to think of Beethoven who was stone deaf, and people said he made all those discords in his music because he could not hear correctly. But Beethoven knew that he intended those discords. He stood by them against the whole world. But you can see that this could not have been very easy.

The unself-confident woman who wrote the farm memory, in skyrocketing up so fast in writing, had one advantage and that was that she has had such a sad and lonely life.[46] But this just gave her a great deal of time to think, for her Imagination to work, and the need to express it, to write it.

But thousands and thousands of people, *all* people, have the same light in them, have their own creative power in them, if they would only come to see it, respect it and let it out.

46. You notice how her childhood memory of the farm was so blissful because of the kindly warm people who were around.

10

Why Women who do too much Housework should Neglect it for Their Writing

This, I found, is the way to get people to writing well, so that they will see how gifted they are and consequently grow in boldness and freedom.

I would ask them to tell about some childhood memory, that is, to write it as carelessly, recklessly, fast and sloppily as possible on paper. It worked for these reasons: they would forget about writing "writing," and about trying to please Teacher. Their only effort became to tell spontaneously, impulsively, what they remembered.

And I asked for *childhood*[47] experiences for this reason. A child experiences things from his true self (creatively) and not from his theoretical self (dutifully), i.e., the self he thinks he *ought* to be. That is why childhood memories are the most living and

47. That is, if they *felt* like writing about their childhood, if they thought it would be interesting. Some prefer other ways of learning.

sparkling and true, like those of the child in the last chapter who, not unkindly, wished that grandpa would die so that she could have the fun of the funeral.

But an older person[48] writing of recent experiences, of things that happened yesterday is continually checked by thinking: "My goodness, how could I ever have such a mean thought about Auntie Mae!" and so puts down: "She was just a dear, old lady with a roguish twinkle in her eyes." Not from the true self and so no good.

A hard-worked, shabby mother of four children came to the class. She wanted to learn to write. She had written (at night, I suppose, after eleven hours of housework) a very long, very bad, lurid novelette, all in a round long-hand on blue-lined writing paper.

Well, I would not think of telling her it was bad (and so commit a murder right there, as so many friends, parents, teachers, editors, employers do, with pleasure and a sense of helpful duty).[49] I found good and living sentences among the dead ones. I spoke of them. I asked her if she would try to write for me some childhood memory: just try that,—carelessly.

This is what she wrote. I have to abridge it somewhat.

* * *

---

48. Until she learns better, unless she discovers her true self and how to write from it.

49. Besides, I have written just as bad ones. Mine have more vocabulary. But she had my weakness, i.e., trying to make a story a tract wherein you prove that "Good will win." I try to show why this is ineffective later.

    And since one's writing always reflects one's personality, as I grow to preach less, and now seem to want to give people something instead of pushing them, I probably will not try to preach in my stories any more,—pushing and forcing my characters this way and that. It is a good thing. Such stories are never any good.

Hurriedly Carolyn slipped out of the heavy flannel night-gown, and shivered as she pulled on the long-sleeved, long-legged underwear, which was clammy from having lain on the floor all night...

A hurried brush of her hair, a clumsy long braid made with stiffening fingers, a search for her hair-ribbon which was gone again. Her teeth began to chatter so she tied her hair with the first thing she found handy, dived into her red-flannel petticoat, snug fitting up to the shoulders to keep her warm, then into the heavy, plaid dress, and down the stairs in a clatter of squeaking steps and bare feet, to put on her shoes by the kitchen fire.

Carolyn was in a hurry, as usual, to get outside in time to hear the early Bells of St. Joseph's church. Her mother busily preparing breakfast, glanced at her to see if she was all together, and noticed one shoe-lace gone.

"Caroline" (Mother never said "Carolyn"), "where is your shoestring?"

"In her hair again, Mama." The answer came from the precise Elizabeth.

"You go right back upstairs, young lady, and get your hair-ribbon."

"But Ma, it's too cold up there."

"You do as I say. And don't forget to wash either."

As Carolyn turned back the covers to look for the ribbon she noticed a small pile of snow on the bed where it had blown in through the cracks under the eaves. She brushed it away and wished she had taken her ribbon off and folded it nicely and placed it on her stand, as Elizabeth always did. Elizabeth never had to hunt for her things in the cold... At last the ribbon was found, kicked tightly against the foot of the bed. It was a sorry sight indeed... She turned to the washbowl. The pitcher was cracked from top to bottom and held upright by the frozen water which had been nice and warm the night before. It must be terribly cold to freeze hard like that, thought Carolyn.

Again she descended the stairs, this time quietly. She took her coat and bonnet from the hook at the foot of the stairs, and slipped silently out the door. Would she still be in time? Yes, there was father waiting beside the barn-door. Then clear it came across the five miles of frozen country. "Bong-bing, Bong-bing." With bowed heads they listened. Clear and loud rang the bells as though they were just beside them, beautifully clear-toned.

"It must be below thirty degrees this morning, the Bells are so loud."

"Do you suppose we will hear Cousin Jeff's sleigh-bells as he comes up the river, Father?"

"We don't usually hear them that far, unless it is more than forty below zero. Listen."

"It's them, it's them," Carolyn clapped her hands in glee. "And they're on the river, Father, hear them?"

"There will be lots of sleds today."

Clearer and clearer came the sound of sleigh-bells, led by the great, round bells which cousin Jeff had on the hames and back of his team. Four on each horse. "Clong-a-long, clang-a-lang" they rang out in mellow beauty above the more silver-toned bells which circled the horses' bodies. Louder and louder they rang as they emerged from the timber-lined, frozen river out onto the open expanse of the lake, up which the farmers hauled to market the wood cleared from their virgin acres. Load after load, a long line of heavy sleds, the squeaking runners mingling their high piercing tones with the tingling bells, proclaimed a bitterly cold morning.

Carolyn's father lived at the half-way bend in the lake. His two sons with their loads would join the long procession as it went by on the long trek to market.

"Father, when it is cold like today, don't you think the sleds sing beautifully?"

She was not quite sure that he would understand her. The sleds going by did something to her inside. She wanted to bottle up all their melodies and keep them. Carolyn had never heard of a symphony, but that was what she heard in the sleds on those cold, cold days.

"Yes, daughter, I love their song."

Carolyn moved closer to him and snuggled her small, ten-year-old hand into his big mittened paw. It was good to have someone understand. Clang-a-lang, jingle-jingle, and the clear song of the sleds, like the tones of a violin, burst forth on the crisp air in all their glory as the sleds swung into view around the bend.

"They are more beautiful than the Bells of St. Joseph's," said Carolyn. "I think that is the way it sounds in heaven."

"Perhaps it is."

"Bong-a-bong." The church bells again led the symphony of sleighs.

"Come, my child, we have been standing here an hour. You will be frozen. Skip along and get ready for school. And don't forget to bundle up warm, because the Bells say forty below."

* * *

You see she writes very well, has a remarkable ear to hear and distinguish beautiful sounds, so much so that she could probably compose music too if she tried to. And you see she had such emotion and clarity about that cold winter morning that we experience it too and know exactly how it was.

And some people's true self is to be funny. A jolly, stoutish woman came to the class. Did she want to write? Well, she had never tried it, she said uneasily and bashfully, hiding behind her fur collar, but she had the queerest feeling that she could be funny.

"Good! Write something. Any old thing."

This is what she brought.

* * *

Mrs. Baker, waiting on a dark corner for a street-car, one wintry night, was becoming frightened. The only other person in sight was a woman who seemed also to be waiting for a car. But this woman appeared to be watching Mrs. Baker much more than any of the oncoming street-cars.

O, why on earth doesn't that woman go home and stop staring at me, thought Mrs. Baker, impatiently. Ever since I was held up last year I can't stand having strangers act interested in what I do, and it makes me simply frantic to hear quick footsteps behind me!

Mrs. Baker put her collar up high around her ears. It was a cold night, with a sharp wind blowing, and little, feathery snowflakes sailing around now and again, finally alighting on the ground and immediately melting. She watched the flakes for awhile, forgetting temporarily the woman.

Then she remembered and suddenly turned, almost knocking over the stranger, who was standing close behind Mrs. Baker now. I do wish that car would come, or that this woman would go some place, thought Mrs. Baker. I would like to have a peek at my wrist watch, but maybe I hadn't better. She might want it, if she saw it, while so far she doesn't know I have one. It must be around eleven o'clock, anyway. How this corner happens to be deserted now, is something I can't understand. Usually so many people are going up and down the sidewalk. Guess I will stroll down to the next corner. My friend or foe, whichever she is, wouldn't dare to follow me. Mrs. Baker walked along briskly, instead of strolling. Half way down the block, when in front of some empty buildings, she became aware of quick footsteps behind her.

Well, if she makes a snatch at my purse, I will just let her have it, decided Mrs. Baker. I couldn't wrestle with a rabbit tonight, to say nothing of that determined-looking woman. If only I knew what is on her mind. It is the uncertainty that bothers me.

Mrs. Baker opened her purse just enough to extract a street-car token from it, and tucked the token in her glove. All I want is to be able to get on that car, if it ever comes, she thought. She walked over to a window and tried to get interested in a jewelry display there. Immediately the woman did the same.

Suddenly Mrs. Baker spied her street-car coming—only a block away. It was as welcome as a gold chariot straight from Heaven. She became very brave, and whirled around and faced the stranger. "Is there something you want of me?" she asked. The woman said, "Are you waiting for the Rice Street car?" Mrs. Baker's inner voice of caution warned her not to tell where she was going, for fear of being followed. She was tired of running away, however, and said, "Yes, I am. It is right here now!" She started to dash out into the street, and the stranger put a detaining hand on Mrs. Baker's arm. "I have been trying to get up nerve enough to speak to you," the woman said. "You see, I have two transfers. I wanted to give you one."

* * *

I think this must surely be funny, because as I read it now I begin to laugh again. I know that I could not read a paragraph of Mrs. Baker's writing without the whole class laughing.

There were many funny people, one of them a very pretty married girl with fine, clear, sleepy eyes and a drawl and a sideways look.[50]

She would begin a story:

"This darned old vacuum cleaner," said old Emma Judkins fretfully shoving it over the parlor rug, "has no more suction than a husband's kiss."

Or:

"I am the rose of Sharon and the lily of the valley!" Reverend Ellison rose from his ecclesiastical rubber heels and rested his narrow hands upon the embroidered cloth that had been presented by the Ladies Sunshine Society of the Evangelical Church."

---

50. So many funny people seem to drawl and be lazy.

She wrote a story called *The Hunt Club Murder*.

Here is the first page:

* * *

The department store tea-room was serving luncheon. Confined by an overstuffed velvet rope, a crowd of women shoppers swayed against one another, shifted their packages from one lumpy hip to the other as they tried to ease their splaying feet, their rubber overshoes wrinkling down at the back under the pressure of ample calves, their glazing eyes fixed on mid-space where floated visionary clouds of whipped cream.

It was noon when the Northwest Drag Hunt club held its weekly luncheon in the Pyramid room. On ordinary days anyone in the main dining room had a clear view of the Pyramid room between the twin columns of wall-board decorated with Egyptian writing that flanked its wide entrance; on Tuesdays the room was made exclusive by a barrier of tall screens and a covert of imitation palms.

Even now the tea room hostess was admitting the club members under the full glare of the waiting proletariat: Mrs. Wheasy, whose three daughters raise hunters to supplement the reduced family income; Mr. Countryman, Master of Hounds, who does his imitation of the English country gentleman on his small estate just outside the city limits; Mrs. Hubbard, whose habit of riding twice a week is like her Southern accent, a hangover from her private school days in Missouri; Roger Hike, leader of the Boy Scout mounted troupe; Miss Olivia O'Hara, whose secondary hobby is the breeding of Schnauzers; Mr. Archibald Feather, still a bachelor by virtue of his discreet preference for devoted wives; Miss Daphne Reno, who is able to keep three hunters on the alimony sent her by a former husband in the east; Dr. Henry Alway, who rides in a futile attempt to keep down his waistline; Miss Vera Clinkit, a private secretary who rides because she thinks it is the "smart thing to do"; and last, Col. Boomer,[51] the president of the organization.

He came charging around the unhooked velvet rope. The disturbed palms swished behind him like grasses through which a running tiger passes. Over his bouillon he observed that the cold weather could not discourage that cad, the obnoxious Archibald Feather. He had never liked the fellow since he had seen him enter the show-ring in an ungodly pair of henna jodhpurs.

Just then Archibald slid down in his chair, his elbows dropping off the table. He jerked suddenly and fell forward until his chin rested on the cloth. Only his head could be seen, eyes closed, like a serving of John the Baptist.

"What's this, Sir?" the Colonel bellowed from his end of the table."... And so on.

Well, from that you can see that this girl is as funny as anyone has ever been. She has two small children, and a husband, and she has hardly written anything at all, and does not think she has any particular ability. I tell her so, but she only half believes it. Like many of the most talented and funniest people, she is too nice and unconceited to work from mere ambition, or the far-away hope of making money, and she has not become convinced (as I have) that there are other reasons for working, that a person like herself who cannot write a sentence that is not delightful and a circus, should give some time to it instead of always doily-carrying, recipe-experimenting, child-admonishing, husband-ministering, to the complete neglect of her Imagination and creative power.

In fact that is why the lives of most women are so vaguely unsatisfactory. They are always doing secondary and menial things (that do not require all their gifts and ability) for *others* and never anything for *themselves*. Society and husbands praise them for it (when they get too miserable or have nervous breakdowns) though

51. These wonderful names!

always a little perplexedly and half-heartedly and just to be consoling. The poor wives are reminded that that is just why women are so splendid—because they are so unselfish and self-sacrificing and that is the wonderful thing about them!

But inwardly women know that something is wrong.[52]

They sense that if you are always doing something for *others*, like a servant or a nurse, and never anything for yourself, you cannot do *others* any good. You make them physically more comfortable. But you cannot affect them spiritually in any way at all. For to teach, encourage, cheer up, console, amuse, stimulate or advise a husband or children or friends, you have to be something yourself. And how to be something yourself? Only by working hard and with gumption at something you love and care for and think is important.

So if you want your children to be musicians, then work at music yourself, seriously and with all your intelligence. If you want them to be scholars, study hard yourself. If you want them to be honest, be honest yourself. And so it goes.

And that is why I would say to the worn and hectored mothers in the class who longed to write and could find not a minute for it:

"If you would shut your door against the children for an hour a day and say: 'Mother is working on her five-act tragedy in blank verse!' you would be surprised how they would respect you. They would probably all become playwrights."

They look at me wistfully and know it is true. But after all these centuries of belief that women should be only encouragers and fosterers of talent in others, and have none of their own (as though you can effectively foster or encourage other people's talent unless you have a great deal of your own!) it is hard to do. I know that. But if women once learn to be something themselves, that

52. Menial work at the expense of all true, ardent, creative work is a sin against the Holy Ghost.

the only way to teach is to be fine and shining examples, we will have in one generation the most remarkable and glorious children.

I have given these very few examples of talent in the class because it is all I have space for. I cannot show you the complete stories, the plays, the slowly-growing novels. But in these few examples of the work of those who had the very least experience of all, you can see that talent does not show forth only in this month's magazines and books, or in the discussed and counter-discussed Broadway stage productions, or in the newspaper syndicated columns, or in literary reviews, or in Hollywood. It is everywhere.

11

Microscopic Truthfulness

Yes, when you get down to the True self and speak from that, there is always a metamorphosis in your writing, a transfiguration. Now I will suggest another way to find your True self. It is what I call writing with "microscopic truthfulness." You might try it if you think you need it.

One of the class was Mrs. B. She had written for many years. She had written a novel (which she had not sold) and many stories. She had truly worked. She was an interesting and competent person, although something about the rather severe, rational, get-down-to-business look through her pince-nez made me feel that it might be a little hard to do much for her. She had taken writing courses and rewritten her "stuff" dozens of times and studied tendencies in magazines and new books and made notes of them and rewritten her novel again in accordance with these tendencies.

I find that I wrote this about her in a letter two years ago.

* * *

My class has started. Timid; all ages. They have turned in some very good things though. In fact it seems to me the only untalented one is a Mrs. B. who has written novels and all kinds of things. But I may be too hard on her. She wants "stiff criticism," she says, and will not be contented unless I am hard on them (which I don't believe in being). Yet she writes herself so externally; "he gripped the chair," etc., etc. And when I tell her to make a point in a story clearer, she wants to know just what to put in it. I tell her that that is her trouble; she thinks of the *words* and not of the story, of the reality of what happened. It does no good to make the words try to sound better, snappier; one must have a clearer idea of the *people* and what happened to them. I am eager to see if this changes her work. I have decided that is why all (except great) fiction is so false, has that queer, bogus sound. "Nancy Flimsy madly swinging her sun hat flew down on the yacht club pier!" But the prominent writers have the same sound in their fiction too, Galsworthy, etc.,—all, it seems to me, but the great Russians.

I tell Mrs. B. and all of them to think of telling a story, not of writing it. When you tell a story then you have the instinctive sense of timing in it, of going into detail where it is important, of moving fast over the surface of the story where that is necessary. No longer the labored dialogue. Well, I talk as though I knew all about it, when I don't and have really just begun, and my own stories have never been much good, God knoweth. But I think I learn more all the time. In writing one must be bold, free and truthful. Being truthful keeps one from the boldness that means showing off (how many Americans do this!).

* * *

Over everything Mrs. B. wrote there was a gloze of the commonplace, a kind of gray, dull, conventionality. Her heroines all tended to be very mean and sinuous and vampish. She loved to write about rather exotically mean people in studio apartments.

Now that is fine. For heaven's sake, if you want to write about mean people, do it. But hers were not quite convincing. They were types.

And you know a "type" is never convincing and never comes to life.

Say that you want to put a Yankee farmer in your story and you want to make him more like a Yankee farmer than any Yankee farmer that ever existed. So you have him look like Uncle Sam and say "Wal, Si," etc. The result? No reader believes him for a second.

But if you did this: if you had once known a Yankee farmer and, conscientiously and in detail, you describe him as the character in your book, even though he is bald, clean-shaven and wears neat business suits, the readers will feel he is true. "There is the most wonderful portrait of a typical Yankee farmer in the book!" they will say.

Yes, the more you wish to describe a Universal the more minutely and truthfully you must describe a Particular.[53]

Well, I told Mrs. B. to write microscopically, truthfully. I told her to describe somebody she knew, to write then, angularly. "Don't try to make it sound smooth and mellifluous, but write with exquisite and completely detached exactness and truthfulness.

---

53. Second rate artists and writers never seem to know this. But the great ones all do. That is why Van Gogh sighed over those who tried to make a picture by half-looking at something, and then from memory making some vague generalization out of it, instead of studying, studying what they painted and showing what they saw and felt about it with all their consummate powers of delicacy and truth.

    Blake wrote:

    "The great and golden rule of art, as well as of life is this: That the more distinct, sharp and wiry the bounding line, the more perfect the work of art; and the less keen and sharp, the greater is the evidence of weak imitation, plagiarism and bungling. Great inventors in all ages knew this. Protogenes and Apelles knew each other by this line. Raphael and Michael Angelo and Albert Dürer are known by this and this alone."

    And he said: "Singular and Particular Detail is the Foundation of the Sublime"; and he said of beautiful forms: "Minuteness is their whole Beauty."

Look at the person and just say what you see, even if it sounds like a catalogue."

Well she did that. She described an old servant—told exactly the shape of her upper lip, the color of her opaque, gray, false teeth, everything.

* * *

The first time she came to see me about helping with the housework, she sat bolt upright in a straight chair and bayoneted me with her black eyes. Her long, upper lip, faintly mustached, drooped to a point in the center. She did not smile easily, but now and then a curious contortion puckered her sallow face. Her year round shapeless hat sat squarely on her smooth white hair. Her uncompromising shirtwaist and full-gored skirt covered her slender, erect body as surely as her indomitable spirit held her amazing years. In eighty-seven years of Spartan living, she evidently had accumulated no dead wood, no adipose tissue...

Although I never freed myself from a feeling of fecklessness under her intent look, I realized as time went on, that she liked me a little. She told me often that she liked men, but that she could not get along with women.

I'll make some gingersnaps if you've got any good molasses," she said one day. "Men like old-fashioned gingersnaps." Fortunately I had the kind she liked, and when everything was assembled, she turned to me. "I want the kitchen to myself now. Just light the oven—I'll make out alone." She closed the door firmly after me. When the aroma of spice and molasses had filled the house for hours, I ventured down to the kitchen. Every available inch of counter room lay thick with cookies. Sarah stood at the window looking out. The expression of her back told me that my appearance was premature. I beat a hasty retreat.

She was delighted when my husband praised her cookies. In her zeal to have him enjoy the lion's share, she hid them from me in the most unlikely places.

Conversation was never easy with her. I had always the feeling of a knight making repeated advances with a flag of truce. She was a feudal turret barred to my entry, but many flying darts from her narrow openings found me.

A life spent for the most part on a stony hill farm in Vermont, had early conditioned her to hard work. With the increasing years, she stood, a little island of isolation, shut away by pride and poverty, poor eyesight and partial deafness, unmoved by the life that swirled about her. Scorning charity in any form, she stood on her own feet to the end, contriving somehow to make us feel under obligation to her.

* * *

This is very good. How can I pontificate with such certainty (like a critic) that it is good? Well, for one thing, the class was astonished and pleased at it. While I read it they all listened with such belief and interest and unswerving attention. Then, everybody seemed to have a bright, exact mental picture of the old servant. I know that this picture has lasted in my mind quite clearly for two years. All this is a sign that it must be good.

So you see, Mrs. B., writing with this exact, cataloguing truthfulness, found her true self, wrote well.

Then there was another strange thing: the change of the personality of the writer,[54] *behind* the words describing the little, old Vermont woman.

If, not knowing Mrs. B., you had read her stories about the sinuous heroines in studio apartments, you would have felt that she, the writer, was an ordinary, untalented person, a shade mean.

---

54. This personality behind the writing I call the Third Dimension. It is very important and I try to tell about it later.

In this new sketch, you would not know she was the same person. You knew the writer was a person of great affection, tenderness and good will, with a fine, bright, sympathetic eye for everything. In other words, in her first stories the unconscious wish to sell, to be sophisticated, to make an impression, weakened them hopelessly, made them commonplace. If she once wrote truthfully, unpretentiously, she tapped in herself a deep source of wisdom, talent and feeling.

And again I say (for surely the hundredth time) this source is in all of you and it is unfathomable.[55]

Another woman's writing changed suddenly when I told her to try being microscopically truthful. She was perhaps sixty years old and lame, a very fine, kind, gentle person. She worked very hard but never seemed to write anything really good and alive.

Finally I said:

"Describe something just as it is. Do not worry if it is angular and clumsy or how it comes out. Just look at something and put down what you see. Remember William Blake who said: 'Improvement makes straight, straight roads, but the crooked roads without improvement are roads of genius.'"[56]

Well, this pupil did as I said. She described a sad, dilapidated, old house. It was startlingly unlike her other writing-graphic and vivid and melancholy. She even noticed colors. She never mentioned a color in her other work.

---

55. Unfathomable, if only you do not forget that your true inner self is ever-changing, ever-creating new things from itself. But if you write one good and successful thing and then try to make all the others just as good, i.e., just like it, then the unfathomable fountain of talent will be dried up.

56. The truth, life itself, is always startling, strange, unexpected. But when the truth is told about it everybody knows at once that it is life itself and not made up.

But in ordinary fiction, movies, etc., everything is smoothed out to seem plausible,—villains made bad, heroes splendid, heroines glamorous, and so on, so that no one believes a word of it.

When I told her how good it was she said:

"But it is so gloomy! I don't like to write depressingly."

I could see then that a lifetime of a kind of *willed* cheerfulness, because of her lameness perhaps, kept her from writing from her true self. "I must be cheerful and optimistic. I must look always at the bright side of everything," she was always saying to herself.

But not when you write! If it is true cheerfulness, fine. But if it is *willed* cheerfulness and you always describe things as you think you *ought* to,—well, it will not be effective, that is all. Nobody will be interested or believe you.

Some people write very solemnly with long words like "co-operation and co-ordination" when their true self is a jolly, vulgar cut-up, full of antics and wise-cracks. In this case if they wrote from the cut-up it would be wonderfully good.

And some hide in an ambush of loud, low-brow humor when their true self is tender-hearted, sensitive, lonely, and romantic.

A young man brought to class always Lardneresque pieces about a man with a neck-shave named Gus and his wife Edna and their raucous, yowling quarrels over lunch money and so on. It was full of belchings, toothpicks, etc., etc. It was not very funny and I began to suspect this was an ambush. I got him to write something that came from himself. "Try not to hide yourself. I would just like to see what you really care about." He said he would try.

He then brought in an episode about a young man who wakes up in the night, out of an uneasy, vaguely wretched dream and thinks that his wife is there in the next bed and is comforted and relieved. Then gradually he remembers: no, she is not there. There is no one in that bed. She has died,—a few days before. It was beautifully written, delicate, tender-hearted, sad. The description of the dream and the struggle to consciousness was perfection. His vocabulary was unrecognizable. There were discriminating, scholarly, exquisitely chosen words.

But how to single out your true self, when we are all so many selves? Yes, I know that is hard. I know I have been much puzzled by this, for I myself seem to be so many different people, sometimes a man, sometimes a woman, a murderer, a whiner, a mother, a simpering lady, an old rip, a minister, a burglar, a lion, a weasel. And all my teaching would go for nothing if, in trying to find your true self, you would begin to strain and cerebrate with an anxious neurasthenic frown: "Am I now writing with the utmost sincerity? I wonder."

No, you must not do that. The only way to find your true self is by recklessness and freedom. If you feel like a murderer for the time being, write like one. In fact, when you are in a fury it is a wonderful time to write. It will be brilliant,—provided you write about what you are furious at, and not some dutiful literary bilge. "Violent Passions emit the Real, Good and Perfect Tones," said Blake.

That is another reason why I think it is a fine thing to write. People who do it, do not ignore any more the bad passions in themselves and shut their eyes to them, ostrichlike, but begin to take a good and interested look at these passions and try to understand them, and are even glad they have them because it has set them thinking. In fact, some passion that everybody has told you was bad—rebelliousness, or obstinacy, or prodigality, say—you may decide is very fine and that you want to keep it.

I have read all of Chekhov now. He is so great, and his letters and his life and what people remember of him is greater. Yet it is consoling that if he did not know all about cruelty, gluttony, cowardice, coldness in himself, he could not have written about them. Great men feel and know everything that mean men feel, even more clearly, but they seem to have made some kind of an ascension, and these evil feelings, though they still understand them sympathetically, no longer exert any power over them.

Gradually by writing you will learn more and more to be free, to say all you think; and at the same time you will learn never to lie to yourself, never to pretend and attitudinize. But only by writing and by long, patient, serious work will you find your true self.[57]

And why find it? Because it is, I think, your immortal soul and the life of the Spirit, and if we can only free it and respect it and not run it down, and let it move and work, it is the way to be happier and greater.

But remember always that the true self is never a fixed thing. You can never say: "Good. Today I find at last what I am really like: splendid type!" You cannot say that because the true self is always in motion like music, a river of life, changing, moving, failing, suffering, learning, shining. That is why you must freely and recklessly make new mistakes—in writing or in life—and do not fret about them but pass on and write more. Active evil is so much better than passive good, which is just docility, feebleness, timidity.

And do not try to be consistent, for what is true to you today may not be true at all tomorrow, because you see a better truth.

---

57. Or by any other art; or by any use of the creative power. Remember always that by "creative power" I mean so much more than what the high-brows call Art. The prize-fighter who works hard and uses his imagination and effort to make himself a better fighter, has it. The woman who looks at a fashion magazine and feels that small gush of pleasurable energy inside: "I might have an evening coat like that and try my hair in a bunch of ringlets above the forehead!" and sees in her imagination the cloak and the curls and how pretty she would look and feels a spring of happy energy as she sets about creating these things,—she has it too.

    The cook wanting to try a new cake has it.

12

Art is Infection

I like the great Russian writers best of all—Tolstoy, Chekhov and Dostoevsky. I think it is because they seemed to feel that truth is more important than all the fancy skillful words, than belles lettres. I, personally, don't like writing where the package is fancier and more important than the contents. Perhaps that is why the Russians translate so well, because the important thing to them is what they felt, saw and thought. Life is more important to them than literature.

The great Russians are the ones who have convinced me that the only way to write well, so that people believe what we say and are interested or touched by it, is to slough off all pretentiousness and attitudinizing. It is much harder to do than you think because our pretentiousnesses are so subtle and often deeply sub-conscious. I want to tell what Chekhov said about this:

In a wonderful story called "A Dreary Story" his hero is an old, sick, disillusioned, great man, a university professor. This is what Chekhov makes him say:

> French books do not satisfy me either, but they are not so tedious as the Russian, and it is not unusual to find in

> them the chief element of artistic creation,—the feeling of personal freedom, which is lacking in the Russian authors. I don't remember one new book in which the author does not try from the first page to entangle himself in all sorts of conditions and contracts with his conscience. One is afraid to speak of the naked body; another ties himself up hand and foot in psychological analysis; a third must have a "warm attitude to man"; a fourth purposely scrawls whole descriptions of nature that he may not be suspected of writing with a purpose... One is bent on being middle-class in his work, another must be a nobleman, and so on. That is intentionalness, circumspection, and self-will, but they have neither the independence nor the manliness to write as they like, and therefore there is no creativeness.

Yes, you must feel when you write, free. You must disentangle all ought's.[58] You must disconnect all shackles, weights, obligations, all duties. You can write as badly as you want to. You can write *anything* you want to,—a six-act blank verse, symbolic tragedy or a vulgar short, short story. Just so that you write it with honesty and gusto, and do not try to make somebody believe that you are smarter than you are. What's the use? You can never be

---

58. I am speaking now of your first drafts. But don't think that writing is not work. Your novel may take eleven years as Tolstoy's "War and Peace" did—rewriting it, seeing the people more clearly in your imagination, polishing it, making it true and more economical of words, working out the bogus and the affected.

    And remember that a fine novel or play is like an iceberg. Some of it is seen but much more of it is not. Someone asked Ibsen how he happened to name the heroine of "A Doll's House" Nora, and he said: "Well, her real name was Eleanora but they got to calling her Nora as a little girl."

    You see, he knew her whole life, everything about her, from earliest childhood, though in the play only a few hours of her life are shown.

    But in first creating a thing I know one must feel free. Everyone's experience in polishing a work may be different. All must learn for themselves, by working.

smarter than you are. You try to be and everybody sees through it like glass, and on top of that knows you are lying and putting on airs. (Though remember this: while your writing can never be brighter, greater than you are, you can hide a shining personality and gift in a cloud of dry, timid writing.)

As you write, never let a lot of "ought's" block you: I *ought* to be more humorous, more Leftist, more like Ernest Hemingway, more bitingly satirical. Then it shows. That spoils it. It will not be alive, but dead.

I know that in my class I could go through some writing and say:

"This sentence is just wonderful. You meant this. This sentence is dead: you were thinking of teacher. It is slag. To thunder with teacher! Write always what you think."

In other words, don't write like an advertising writer. I have often thought how billions of dollars are spent on advertising in this country. Advertising companies hire the very brightest, wittiest young people to write for them. Not one single sentence of it is worth repeating. Why? Because it wasn't meant. It was all written, not because the writer felt something and then said it (if you feel a thing the more simply you say it the better, the more effective), but because he tried to impress and inveigle people, convince them something is very fine about which he himself does not really care a button.

An imprisoned tinker named Bunyan[59] can write a thing with one set and arrangement of words. John Keats can write a thing with a very different set and arrangement of words. Both are great

---

59. All prisoners should write. It would be good for them and good for us. Some of the greatest literature has been written by prisoners, among them Sir Walter Raleigh, Bunyan and Dostoevsky.

Prisoners suffer, think and are alone, so they have very much to say. Their creative yearning and power is shown by the fact that there is much more demand for great literature in prisons than outside. A librarian told me this.

literature because a great man thought these things and said them as accurately and honestly as he could.

I was very much helped by something Tolstoy said about writing. I tell you because it may help you. First he said that there is nothing in the world that should not be expressed in such a way that an affectionate seven-year-old boy can see and understand it. I often think of this and it is a guide and help.[60] I take down a book by Tolstoy and see that he does as he advocates.

Then in a famous essay called "What is Art?" (which made everybody very angry) he said something like this: Art is infection. The artist has a feeling and he expresses it and at once this feeling infects other people and they have it too. And the infection must be *immediate* or it isn't art. If you have to puzzle timidly over a picture or book, and try, *try* to like it and read many erudite critics on the subject so that you can say at last: "Yes, I think I really do begin to understand it and see that it is just splendid! Real art!" Then it is not Art.[61]

Tolstoy said this:

> The business of art lies just in this,—to make that understood and felt which, in the form of an argument, might be incomprehensible and inaccessible...
>
> And such has always been the nature of good, supreme art; the "Iliad," the "Odyssey,"... the Hebrew prophets, the gospel parables, and the hymns of the Vedas; all transmit very elevated feelings and are nevertheless comprehensible to us now, educated and uneducated; as they were comprehensible to the men of times long ago who were even less educated than our laborers...

---

60. Of course if *your* creative impulse, your true self, tells you to write elaborately and complexly, then you must do so.

61. Though it might be Art to others who would see it and be immediately infected.

> The hindrance to understanding the best and highest feelings (as is said in the gospel) does not at all lie in deficiency of development or learning.[62] A good and lofty work of art may be incomprehensible, but not to simple, unperverted peasant laborers[63] (all that is highest is understood by them)... For instance, I know people who consider themselves most refined, and who say that they do not understand the poetry of love to one's neighbor, or self-sacrifice, or of chastity.
>
> So that good, great, universal art may be incomprehensible to a small circle of spoilt people, but certainly not to any large number of plain men.

Great art, said Tolstoy, is when a great man who has the highest life-conception of his time tells what he feels. (Tolstoy himself was one of these although he did not know it.) Then the infection is universal. *Everybody* understands it and at once.[64]

But besides true art, said Tolstoy, there is a great deal of imitation art, pseudo-art. This is because rich people are bored and idle and must be entertained, and so they pay artists to amuse them by making art for them. But since art must be truly felt and cannot

---

62. So said Blake:

"Jesus supposes everything to be Evident to the Child and to the Poor and Unlearned. Such is the Gospel.

"The whole Bible is filled with Imagination and Visions from End to End and not with Moral Virtues; that is the baseness of Plato and the Greeks and all Warriors. The Moral Virtues are continual Accusers of Sin and promote Eternal Wars and Dominancy over others."

I think he means that the Moral Virtues assume they know best what is good for people, while Jesus with His love and Imagination knew that each must be allowed to grow freely and in his own way.

63. Blake. "Who does not know the Truth at Sight is unworthy of Her Notice."

64. I think Blake meant this same thing too, when he called Jesus an artist.

be *willed,* since it has to generate spontaneously in the artist's inner self, there comes into existence a lot of willed, brain-spun pseudo-art. And one common kind of pseudo-art is that which pretends to be very hard to understand, subtle and abstruse, so that only a very exclusive few, a few extremely cultured people, can understand it.

And so there arise critics to explain art. But critics, Tolstoy said, are people especially incapable of knowing what art is because "they are erudite, that is perverted, and at the same time very self-confident individuals." All that erudition, weighing, measuring, reasoning and comparing, spoils these critical people, makes them opaque and atrophied so that they cannot *feel* any more with the immediacy of a child or of plain people or of poets.

That is why: "Critics have always been men less susceptible than other men to the contagion of art." And this is shown by the fact, Tolstoy says, that they try to *explain* and interpret Art, when an artist's work is a thing that cannot be interpreted or explained by words because it is infection.

He then tells of another kind of pseudo-art. It comes about like this. Say that you are infected by a book. So you say: "These very moving things—I think I will write about them in my book too." But it is no go. You cannot move people by a second-hand infection.

> "Some forty years ago," Tolstoy wrote, "a stupid but highly cultured lady (since deceased) asked me to listen to a novel written by herself. It began with a heroine who, in a poetic white dress, and with poetically flowing hair, was reading poetry near some water in a poetic wood. The scene was in Russia but suddenly from behind the bushes the hero appears, wearing a hat with a feather a Ia Guillaume Tell (the book specially mentioned this) and accompanied by two poetical white dogs... But as soon as the gentleman

began to converse with the maiden in the white dress, it became obvious that the authoress had nothing to say, but had merely been moved by poetic memories of other works... But an artistic impression, i.e., infection is only received when an author has, in a manner true to himself, experienced the feeling which he transmits and not when he passes on another man's feeling, previously transmitted to him."

When I read this in Tolstoy it seemed like a great flashing discovery. But perhaps I would not have been so struck by it if it had not been for my class. I saw in their writing how whenever a sentence came from the true self and was felt, it was good, alive, it infected one no matter what the words were, no matter how ungrammatical or badly arranged they were. But when the sentence was not felt by the writer, it was dead. No infection.

This helped me because it showed me there is no sense in writing anything I don't feel; or working up a lot of bogus feelings, because nobody will be one bit impressed or affected. But, as I told the people in my class, you must not think of a feeling as necessarily a violent and terrific thing,—"harsh, dry sobs," and so on. Boredom is a feeling, lassitude is a feeling, sleepiness is a feeling as well as rage.

And so from now on, if you want to write, for example, about a man who is suffering from boredom, just quietly describe[65] what your own feelings are when you have been bored. This is all you have to do. Don't say the boredom was "agonizing, excruciating," unless your own boredom was, which is doubtful.

That is all you have to do to infect, to convince your reader, to make him think it is a good description, because it seems true.

---

65. The more delicacy there is in your perceptions of how boredom feels, the better writing it will be. But don't forget that your impulsive, free way of saying it will be better, closer, truer than the planned, contrived way.

13

The Third Dimension

And that is why, if you are writing stories, you must never be an advocate of your characters. Never be saying (in so many words), "See what a fascinating heroine this is, how adorable; how fine and brave the hero!"

Now this would be all right if it were effective. But the trouble is the more you try to *say* your heroine is wonderful, the more your readers will look at her dubiously. They know you are lying in a way, that you really don't see her clearly in your imagination as an actual and living person, but you are trying to put her over on them; you are a propagandist for her. And the more you describe her adorable traits, the more they will just have the unpleasant feeling that the writer is a self-adoring prig.

In "The Possessed" Dostoevsky describes a famous writer, one of the characters in the novel. Dostoevsky says:

> "He described the wreck of some steamer on the English coast, of which he had been the witness, and how he had seen the drowning people saved and the dead bodies brought ashore. All this rather long and verbose article was

written solely with the object of self-display—One seemed to read between the lines: 'Concentrate yourselves on me—Behold what I was like at those moments. What are the sea, the storm, the rocks, the splinters of wrecked ships to you? I have described all that sufficiently to you with my mighty pen. Why look at that drowned woman with the dead child in her dead arms? Look rather at ME, see how I was unable to bear that sight and turned away from it. Here I stood with my back to it, here I was horrified and could not bring myself to look; I blinked my eyes,—isn't that interesting?'"

I have so often been troubled by my own stories, especially those I wanted to be particularly pure Art, earnest and uncompromising.[66] All the characters in them (except the villain) would seem to be ME and it might be read like this:

"I love you," said Brenda Ueland to Brenda Ueland.

"I love you too," Brenda answered shyly, with a sincere look in her fine, strong face.

I read many stories in the magazines like that. The author need not be a hopelessly conceited ass either, but is often quite nice. I think it happens because such writers are not writing truthfully and objectively, but trying to put something over, to prove dishonestly and indirectly to the reader that their characters are so splendid. And that is propaganda, advertising writing, and not the truth.

No, the characters must come fully to life in your imagination. Then objectively and accurately tell just how they looked and

66. That is why you must not *try* too hard to be honest, sincere, in your writing, for that too is a kind of falseness. When you are honest there is no *trying* about it. You are just quietly honest and that is all there is to it.

what they did. If they were fascinating and adorable, it will show. And it will be believed. But always try to write honestly. If you want to say that Fascism is terrible, don't write a novel to prove it, for readers will feel: "These are not real people in this book but a lot of conversing types, pushed about to prove that Fascism is terrible."

No, it would be more effective, instead of the novel, to write straight, honest exposition and tell just why Fascism is terrible. For in fiction, Chekhov said, you can pose a question (about poverty, morality, or whatever it is) but you must not answer it. As soon as you answer it the readers know you are lying, i.e., forcing your characters to prove something.

But, you will say, the great Russians were propagandists in their novels, that no writers in the world were such terrifically effective propagandists. But I answer that in this way: it was not because they shoved their characters about to illustrate this or that social theory. No, these writers, in their honesty, earnestness and extraordinary clear vision, saw some people and what happened to them, and told it. And the books, whether it was "Resurrection" or "The Brothers Karamazov," or Chekhov's stories, were great and unforgettable because the reader feels throughout:

"These people exist. I shall never forget them. And the writer of this book,—this great, this wise, this compassionate man, this man incapable of lying to himself or to anybody else, sees life in this way. And he does not tell us didactically and gloomily, like a learned pessimist, or with meanness and jeering like a satirist, how it should be different, but in every sentence we feel it, just the same."

And in every sentence, no matter what horror, evil and misery a truly great book may describe, I know that I seem to have a feeling of wonderful gratitude and hope (really and literally I can hardly read a Chekhov or Tolstoy without a kind of obstruction in my throat of grateful emotion), for I say to myself: at least there has lived in the world a great man like this writer,—too great to be a brilliant know-it-all, too kind to be a satirist. If this is so, I am glad I live in this world too and believe in God and all His creations.

The ordinary writer may describe poverty and tell even worse and more noisome details than there are in Dostoevsky, say. One reads it with a touch of morbid interest and faint disgust but no other impression is made. No light or love is thrown on poverty at all, and you feel no concern over it and no anguish that such things exist and no illumination as to how we must all be different from now on.

"This writer," you know inwardly, "is more concerned about writing some 'stark realism,' than about poverty. He says 'whore' a great many times to show you how outspoken he is and does not intend to mince matters."

But since he has no true feelings about poverty, nothing to offer about it, neither do you, the reader, have any feelings about it. There is no infection.

Chekhov wrote this letter to his brother:

> You have only one defect... your extraordinary lack of education... Educated people in my opinion must satisfy the following conditions:
>
> 1. They respect a man's personality, and therefore are always tolerant, gentle, polite, yielding. They do not make a riot about a little hammer or a lost rubber; living with others they do not make a favor of it, and when leaving do not say, "It is impossible to live with you!" They excuse noise, and cold, and over-roasted meat, and witticisms, and the presence of other people in their house...
>
> 2. They are compassionate, and not only with beggars and cats, for they grieve in their soul for what the naked eye does not see... They do not sleep for nights so as to help their parents pay for their brothers' studies, to buy clothes for their mother...

3. They respect other people's property and therefore they pay their debts.

4. They are pure in heart and fear a lie as they fear fire. They do not lie, even in trifles. A lie is humiliating to the listener, and it debases the speaker before his own eyes. They do not show off; they behave in public just as they behave at home; they do not throw dust in the eyes of humbler people, and do not make up soul-to-soul conversations when they are not asked. Out of respect for other people's ears they are often silent.

5. They do not belittle themselves to arouse the compassion of others. They do not play on the strings of other people's souls so that they shall sigh over and fondle them. They do not say: "People do not understand me!" because all this produces a cheap effect; it is vulgar, musty, false.

6. They are not vain-glorious. They do not care about such false diamonds as acquaintanceship with celebrities, shaking hands with the drunken P—, the raptures of a well-met fellow at the salon, popularity in public houses... Doing a farthing's worth, they do not walk about with their brief cases as if they had done a hundred roubles' worth, and do not boast of having been admitted where others are not admitted.

From this (though Chekhov is not writing about himself) you know all about him. You do not need to read a biography of him. In fact you know what he is from one sentence, or a fragment of a sentence, such as "They are compassionate, and not only with beggars and cats, for they grieve in their soul for what the naked eye does not see."

The personality behind the writing is so important. This is what I call the Third Dimension. On the paper there are all the neatly written words and sentences. It may be completely objective, with

"I" not written there once. But behind the words and sentences, there is this deep, important, moving thing—the personality of the writer. And whatever that personality is, it will shine through the writing and make it noble or great, or touching or cold or niggardly or supercilious or whatever the writer is.

The words on the paper may be as opulent as Shakespeare's and learned and witty. If the writer's personality is peevish, cold or whatever it is, it will show through. And the words and sentences on the paper may be ungrammatical, bromidic, low-brow, commonplace. If the Third Dimension, the writer's personality, has something fine in it, there you will see it through the inept, dull words, as through glass.

A little servant girl was in my class. She was sickly, pale, wore glasses and had poor teeth. She timidly apologized for not coming to the class oftener, and for not turning in more writing, but the lady she worked for did not like it very well when she went out in the evening.

Twice she sent me through the mail on tiny scraps of paper, something written in pencil. Here is one of them:

HURRY! HURRY!

By Miss Lee Frisbie

> Rushing thru the kitchen getting dinner, then the serving, waiting on fussy tots and the numerous little tasks that must be done. Then the dishes stacks of them, tidying up the kitchen, getting the tots off to dreamland then guess what the time may be. Only 9 after a hard day's work should of been thru an hour ago. Hurry! Hurry! when you hurry so fast you just can't hurry any more. I heard that word so much that it's bore some to hear it ever again.

> I'd really like to walk down town some day and really mosey along at any rate of speed desired and hear the word ringing in my ears, "Idle, idle," instead of "Hurry, Hurry"—and even though no cash to spend just go window shopping.

You see she just wrote hastily a few sentences that happened to be in her soul, and so I feel what she feels. I am infected. And if we take Tolstoy's criterion this is Art. And I think it is too. I think it is very beautiful and much better than many poems in the magazines, for these reasons:

What this girl feels I feel. What her whole life is I know. I find myself much more stirred up imaginatively about the situation of servants than I am by the bitter, trenchant articles of Leftists, or by the grave studies of sociologists. I find myself utterly enraged that in our system, patient, gentle creatures give sixteen hours of their day to someone else, for four or five dollars a week, and that everybody thinks it is all right. I am not only moved but I am eternally changed, for I shall henceforth never exploit a servant.

And so I am sure this tiny piece of unpunctuated writing is a poem, is Art. Dostoevsky would think so too. You have only to read his great novel, "Poor People," to see this.

And that is why I have come to think that the only, way to become a better writer is to become a better person. By better I do not mean goody-goodier, for a great person often does things that so-called good people think very bad indeed. And I have come to think there is irony in the lives of writers who sit at a desk always, tenderly or crossly protecting themselves from all disturbances, danger or uncomfortableness, so that they can work out a better literary style.

Tolstoy, Ibsen, Blake, Goethe, Thomas Mann and all great men, known or unknown, famous or obscure,—they are great men in the first place and so they cannot say anything that is not important, not a single word. Their writing, their art is merely a by-product, a cast-off creation of a great personality. And that is why I think we should all, great and small, be creating all the time, casting off our works but forgetting them, and looking always toward the work ahead. For only by seeing that our creations are vulgar and mean can we see what our souls are, and then, by our Imagination, see how to be better.

I picked up Tolstoy lately, "Resurrection," and those Russians again! Now every word they write in a mysterious way is autobiographical and *true* and yet when they write about repulsive people, whom no doubt they knew well, there is nothing caddish or reprehensible about it, as there is when other writers describe living people in their books. Why is that? Is it because Tolstoy and Chekhov and Dostoevsky and Gorky were so serious, so impassioned, so truthful about everything and would never let themselves show off or jeer or exaggerate? If you are serious in describing bad people and not mean or derisive or superior (i.e., if you are a great man) even the bad people will be grateful. I would never resent being described by Chekhov, no matter how repellent the picture. I would try to be better. If Sinclair Lewis did it, or D. H. Lawrence or H. L. Mencken I would sue for libel,—a million dollars.

T. E. Lawrence, for example, writes "The Seven Pillars of Wisdom" and it is a work of genius, and the beauty of his writing has not been seen in English for a long time. I think it is because of the Third Dimension, the great personality of Lawrence behind it. Instead of living a sedentary, literary life, assiduously polishing sentences and cultivating a prose style, he lived a great life with supernatural standards for himself of courage, suffering, endurance and honor. And so his book is better writing than the books of a century of merely literary men.

Lawrence seems to me like an Elizabethan Englishman, and his writing has the same quality. And this is my theory about it: in Elizabeth's time, during the Renaissance, people felt that the *personality* was the important thing, not a man's ideas alone or his work. A man must be what they called "l'uomo universale," a complete man. That is, a man of action was supposed also to have a soul and be tender-hearted and have delicate, aesthetic sensibilities and to look handsome and to be able to write poetry and music and to paint. And a philosopher or scholar could not be a dry, sedentary pedant but must also be physically fine looking and as athletic and brave as a soldier. They even thought that women should be both learned and beautiful, never just one or the other.[67]

But now we are apt to say of a man: "Oh, you must not pay any attention to his *personality*; it is his ideas that are the important thing."

But I think—and so did Socrates and Michelangelo and many others—that the ideas of a meager and dishonest personality are no good. They are corrupt somewhere. And most important of all, if he has good ideas, but is not good *himself* there is no infection; nobody will be really affected by his ideas, enkindled or changed.

67. Though I think that women to be complete should be physically strong and agile too.

14

Keep a Slovenly, Headlong, Impulsive, Honest Diary

Now this is an inevitable truth: whatever you write[68] will reveal your personality, and whatever you *are* will show through in your writing.

The same thing happens in painting. Leonardo da Vinci said this long ago. He said that just as a man's soul (insistently creative) creates his body, in the same way if the man paints a portrait, it will always look like himself, the painter, as well as the sitter. You have only to buy a dollar's worth of pastels and draw somebody to discover this.

In the class there was a young woman with thick black hair, bright color, clear handsome green eyes, a broad grin, a deep voice, a hearty baritone laugh so volatile and ready to burst out that it hung by a thread. She wore stylish clothes and looked as dashing as a Cossack.

Well, this is what she wrote, her first effort:

68. That is when you learn to write freely and truly and not as the teachers told you to.

She was seated in the front of the car beside him.

"Every summer vacation when school is dismissed" she told him "Father drives us to our cottage at the lake."

"How did you come to be stationed at Sand Lake" she inquired.

"With the advent of the New Deal" he explained—"I enlisted in the conservation work and as a result of years spent in the U. S. Forest Service I was made superintendent of the camp."

"Oh that's wonderful!" she praised.

"Tell me more about the camp" she begged. "What other activities besides the usual camp routine?"

"From time to time" he informed "We have different entertainments sponsored by various civic organizations." Adding "We are having a camp festival and dance soon."

"Would you be interested in attending" he asked.

Enthused her dark eyes shining "Oh, thanks, I'd love to."

Kemp was pleased. He liked this wholesome and frank mannered young girl.

They were near the city where the Cardozos lived. He swung the car around to the street where Addie's home was located. He stopped in front of the house and helped them in getting the luggage out of the car.

Again and again the excited group expressed thanks to their rescuer. In turn he smiled broadly. His even white teeth, showed a deep contrast to his tanned face.[69]

---

69. I could tell her that this was a good sentence. Somehow I felt she really saw his face when she wrote this. Having such healthy color herself and level strong short teeth naturally she would notice them in others, and describe them in a living sentence.

> Addie turned to wave farewell, as he drove away. She felt in her heart that she and this likeable fellow were going to spend many happy days together.

But I knew of course that this writing was not what she *could* write, just from one look at her. To look at her I knew that her writing would be good because it would be like her: jolly, handsome, loud-laughing and slightly ribald. Because she had vitality and bright colors in her complexion and wore bright colors, I knew that she could *see* bright colors and they would sparkle in her writing, and so would her jokes and her stylishness. In fact as I read a sentence or two of this piece aloud, she had a hard time throttling her horror and her bass laugh, though she had written it seriously and tried to make it as good, as much like literature, as she possibly could.

Presently she was writing as well as I knew she would be. It began to be full of color and rowdy and very, very good. She got more of her true self out on paper.

Now to get to writing the truth, i.e., what you really feel, and to speak it straight out, tearing aside all gauzes and films of circumspection or intentionalness or gentility or assumed brutality[70] if you do not know what this means now, write twenty more stories and a true, careless, slovenly, impulsive, honest diary every day of your life, and you will. And you must in time learn to write from your true self not only in your letters and diary, but in fiction. "For a lie is even more annoying in a story than in conversation," said Chekhov. Perhaps I can explain crudely what this means.

A girl in my class once described a young man, her hero, by saying: "His muscles rippled through his shoulders."

I turned to her and said:

---

70. The he-man pose is just as much of a pose as a sissified refinement. We think of hypocrites as pretending to be doves. But they also pretend to be eagles and lions.

"Are you sure they really rippled? They so often ripple in fiction, but have you ever seen that? Can you see this young man clearly in your imagination? Can you tell me what he looked like?"

She said very earnestly:

"Yes, I can. And they *did* ripple. His shoulders were very big and looked as if they would burst through the seams in his coat."

"Well," I said, "put that down. That is just wonderful, a fine graphic description."

When you say in fiction: "He bowed his head in shame," it is likely to be a lie. Or "he gripped the chair until his knuckles were white." When you write such a thing about a character, ask yourself: "Did he really do that? Have I ever seen *anyone* do that?" If you really have and it is true and you see this character do it in your inner vision of his story, put it down. Then it will be all right.

When you have written a story and it has come back a few times and you sit there trying to write it over again and make it more impressive, do not try to think of better *words*, more gripping words. Try to see the people better. It is not yet deeply enough imagined. See them—just what they did and how they looked and felt. Then write it. If you can at last see it clearly the writing is easy.

But the main thing is to discover the real. You, not the bogus literary You who get "A" in your English courses.

Unless you are a very clear-sighted and introspective person, this is a long discipline. The way to do it is, Dostoevsky said: "Never, never lie to yourself. Don't lie to others, but least of all to yourself." "What do you really care about and love? Who are you?" And one of the very worst, self-murdering lies that people tell to themselves is that they are no good and have no gift and nothing important to say.

Don't be afraid of writing bad, mawkish stories for that will show you many things about yourself, and your eye and taste and what you really feel and care about will become clearer to you. If you write a bad story, the way to make it better is to write three more. Then look at the first one. You will have grown in understanding, in honesty. You will know what to do to it. And to yourself.

That is why I think it is good to keep a diary. I don't mean a "had lunch" diary. But do this: write every day, or as often as you possibly can, as fast and carelessly as you possibly can, without reading it again, anything you happened to have thought, seen or felt the day before.

In six months look at it. A drawer full of paper will have accumulated. You will see that what you have written with the most slovenly freedom—in those parts there will be vitality, brilliance, beauty.

By being so careless, by taking it off on paper as fast as you can, you will not write what is dutiful and boring to you. You will not lumberingly over-explain, as they all do in political speeches and articles on economics. You will go straight to the point-be awkward, quick, insolent. Oh, this over-explaining! It is the secret of all boredom. It is like this: You, the writer, go slowly and laboriously with many words, while the reader gropes through it, saying impatiently: "Yes, yes, hurry, hurry up! I see it—I get it! Go on to the next."

The secret of being interesting is to move along as fast as the mind of the reader (or listener) can take it in. Both must march along in the same tempo. That is why it is good to read your writing aloud to yourself. As soon as your voice drags, cross that part out.

It is just as when you listen to a politician making a speech:

"Yes, yes!" you say to yourself impatiently as his voice pounds on, "'Democracy.' I know it. I get it. I see the point you are going to make fifteen minutes from now: you are going to say—'Democracy is a fine thing!'"

And so you stop listening to the hammering voice, falsely inflated with eloquence, since the speaker's own interest in the subject is artificial, and think of other things and yawn and wish he would make an end.

But when you are interested in a speech or something written, there is a pull-along every second. You wait for each phrase, each quick, new idea, gratefully and eagerly, as it comes.

When I was a staff writer on a magazine several years ago, and set to work on an article, I would write laboriously (and with what ennui! What struggle to pin my attention on it!) ten or twelve pages. I would realize then that I had just explained very elaborately and with a great deal of rewriting and polishing, something that everybody knew already. With a sigh and as though throwing off a great weight, I would say to myself angrily:

"What in thunder do you want to say?"

"That women are too fat," my true self[71] answered immediately and in a flash.

"Well, put that down," I said to myself. And so I did, and it was right.

And so in your diary, if you write fast, as though you vomited your thoughts on paper,[72] you will touch only those things that

---

71. The true self is really the Conscience (or Holy Ghost). Your reason may wrangle and argue with you by the hour: "On the one hand, if I do a little of this sort of thing it will be good and a help in the long run and they say it is only natural, and perhaps I really need this sort of thing more in my life"; and so on and so on. But you ask your Conscience at last the blunt question: "What shall I do?" "Go right home and to bed!" it says like a shot.

    But remember I do not mean by the Conscience morality or convention, or the "still small voice that tells you somebody is looking." That sort of conscience may tell you to be a dejected duty-doing citizen, living with your wife, while your true Conscience may tell you to elope with someone else,—that in that only is there truth and bravery and the greater life.

72. This is a device to help you find your true self. When you find it and see how gifted you are, you can write as slowly as you want to.

interest you. You will skip from peak to peak. You will sail over the quagmire of wordy explanations and timidly qualifying phrases.

And know this: whenever you find yourself writing a single word or phrase or page dutifully and with boredom, then leave it out. Something is wrong. It is dragged in. It isn't your true self talking. If what you write bores you, it will bore other people. They will have hard going over it and the sleigh-runners of their attention will grind on squeaking, bare dirt.

I have kept such a slovenly, headlong, helter-skelter diary for many years. I have written in it, off and on, and sometimes in exact detail and as minutely and accurately as the Recording Angel. Horrible things (that I did not know about myself) are revealed in it but perhaps remarkable things too. It has been a great help to me. This is what it has done for me:

It has shown me that writing is talking, thinking, on paper. And the more impulsive and immediate the writing the closer it is to the thinking, which it should be.

It has made me like writing. For years it was the most boring, dreaded, and effortful thing to do-doubt-impeded, ego-inflated.

It has shown me more and more what I am—what to discard in myself and what to respect and love.

Here I will quote from it. For I want to show you that things written in five or three or half a minute are interesting and pretty good. I can typewrite nearly as fast as I think. This is a help. It makes the involuntary spilling of one's thinking more possible.

I select more interesting and brighter parts of my diary. There is much in it that is mere slag—about my digestion, about long, tiresome soul struggles (tiresome even to me now). Yes, there is much boring self-absorption in it. But that is the fine thing about a diary: I do not bother to do it so much now, thanks to this record of it.

February 6, 1936. Wednesday

University. Miss N. that beautiful poor dirty intellectual stupid girl. And Mr. G. and I can't bear to let her get a run of talk; so like middle west, the kids talking, me... "sort a kinda kin' a sort a *you* know a soldier or sump'm." And as she talks puts long hands with cylindrical oval nails a half-inch longer than tapering fingers and slips these in and out of neck of greasy rayon dark blue dress, pulling up dress shields, and jerking at chemise and arm pits and when she stands, twitches and pulls skirt and long heavy knot of hair hanging way down on neck, and high on head a gritty tinsel toque of some sort that looks like a magic mit from Kresge's, one of those things you scrape pots and pans with in washing dishes. Yet such a pretty face, Victorian beauty, lovely teeth and fine gray eyes; a sunken bust, long neck, and figure that begins to swell and droop half way to the waist, and swells more and more, like a bottle or stalactite as approaches the ground. Heavy legs and toes out and has on vici-kid shoes with high cuban heels, and comes flipping down the halls—walks like a seal, a kind of gallop, flippity flopping, her feet come slapping down, turning way out.

March 15th 1935

I took a walk before dinner yesterday (every day I must do this; to walk when one is empty, hungry—not strainingly but easily and feeling the wind in the nostrils, that is always an experience; one really hears the March wind, has that sense of clear transparent translucent BEING.) I have been having interesting arguments with George, Jim, Joe Beach, all are against me, on the question of religion. They are all, and so glad of it, atheists, materialists... And kind generous people, but without religion; all their passion is a negative thing, a minus sign (i.e., indignation vs. the bad, not love of what is better) indignation against unfair wage scale, Wm. R. Hearst, crooked politicians, the fact that we do not enter the World Court, etc., and their Plus then (what they love admire and want) is just hedonism,—that is, the good life to them then is just comfort, affection, happy friends, frolicksome children and cozy warm love-making with one's wife... But to the religious ones (I wish I could be one) the PLUS is glory and fire and the mighty wind and wild music of the spheres, n.b., Blake, Scriabin, John Fox, Bach, Shelley, Thomas More, Milton, Nietzsche, Tolstoy and all the innumerable ones... Now sans religion we are creatures of duty, we go from this to that and try patiently to do it creditably, take good care of our children, be kind and just to all, win law cases etc. but one does not do MORE than that. The soul (said Plato and others) was something that was *self* starting... the First Mover Unmoved. Those who have had religion (true religion, not just orthodox) were incandescent and a thousand times more than merely good and dutiful. Well, so we argue... all this started out of my reading Jung.

January 20th 1935

Up at seven and at 7:30 to Mari's wedding in this dim soft white snow. Lovely early light, almost murk, the world is so softly white like ermine... The little church tower... over the snowy walks, the murky altar lighted by a tender sparkle, sprinkling of candles... The spectacled priest with his white satin chasuble, the little boys, three of them, dark childish heads out of starched white and lace and cardinal red. Kneeling, ringing bells, kneeling, genuflecting up and down busily in their dresses but dark hobbledehoy shoes kicking out from the lace... Mari and bridegroom and two others kneel in front throughout. Long long service, half hour and more... at last priest gets to open the golden door to the grail... Then many parishioners come up, heavy, worn clumsy workmen, teamsters, in thick layers of dirty and frayed overcoats and move up to the railing and kneel down and open their mouths one after the other like bird lings, to get the wafer. The little boy follows the priest like a helpful child and holds under each proffered wafer, a golden mirror, so no crumbs will fall perhaps... Then these quietly and clumsily return to the church, down the aisles, large horny hands, coarse seamed callous faces and great paunches (on one) come down the aisles, red swollen hands gently held before them in a point, in prayer point. "How do you like it?" I say to Roy Jones. "I always weep," he said.

This is a good description. As I read it now I am surprised and elated at myself. If you keep such a diary you will be as pleased with yourself,—and more surprised. Because all people see and feel things sparklingly but it is all dulled or lost before it gets out on paper.

In my diary I often say things about writing.

November 5, 1935

My agent sent back the one story of mine that he had. I wrote it last winter. I looked at it. It is just awful. Such conceit, such railing, such lack of study of the object one is writing about... When I read again the egocentric boring stuff that I have written it is a silly work. I will allow myself some time to let it get better. But one shouldn't be allowed such indulgence forever. Still it is a lot of fun and very absorbing.

July 12, 1934

It seems to me it is my vanity that makes me a bad writer and ashamed to have people see what I do, that in writing the show-off in me veils my insight and observation. It is the same way in listening to music; if I suppress the conceited egocentric, then I really begin to hear the music in a vast flood and understand it; if I do the same when I talk to people then I hear them so much better, what they are saying and see into them so much farther. But experiment, experiment; theory, theory. I may be talking nonsense.

December 18, 1936

What I told M. about having a "thin talent" was not the dumps at all, but a realization that expecting too much of myself means one is afraid of work, does not enjoy it, has too much sorrow when it is bad, and it also means all this involuted perfectionism from which I often suffered so much, working things over—too fussy-mussy.

Now it is not that I don't believe in working things over, but I believe one can *dwell* on a thing too much and when the working over is, so much of it, because of some fear of being caught a fool by the public,—that is a mistake. So I said to M. (and she did not understand) that I now say to myself: "You may not have much ability but what you have, get it all out and be humble and simple and work even if you can think of no words with more than one syllable, and do the best you can and learn by doing *much much*, in spite of imperfections."

It is like Francesca not letting one learn the Merry Farmer perfectly, by months of practice but instead, having us play badly and with enthusiasm *all* of Beethoven, Bach, etc. For inside one always there is the inevitable impulse toward perfection, as much as one is capable of. So there is no sense in niggling over details, if it is a kind of prissy fear. To work to get nearer the truth, that is all right. But only work and feeling free will bring that out—what perfection there is in one.

> Yes, from writing a diary I am sure that I have learned things. But I don't think the learning process would have moved on so well, if I had not written down today's minute revelation. And that is why, if you want to write, you might try it.

15

You do not Know What is in You—an Inexhaustible Fountain of Ideas

Another reason for writing a diary is to discover that the ideas in you are an inexhaustible fountain. "No communications and no gifts can exhaust genius," said Lavater. No human being, as long as he is living, can be exhausted of his ever changing, ever moving river of ideas. We are so apt to think of ourselves as a stomach with arms and legs and a skein of nerves in the skull, which sometimes, when we have plenty of sleep and some hot coffee, seems to give off a few ideas.

But to write happily and with self-trust you must discover what there is in you, this bottomless fountain of imagination and knowledge.

In Plato's dialogue, "The Meno," Socrates talks to a young Thracian aristocrat named Meno, and they discuss whether anything can be taught; that is, does a person when he is taught, learn something *new* or just recollect what he knew already, what his soul learned in former states of being.

Socrates calls to Meno's little slave boy, a child without education.

> "Attend now, Meno," Socrates says, "to the questions which I ask him, and observe whether he learns of me, or only remembers... Tell me, boy, do you know that a figure like this is a square?" (Socrates draws it for him).
>
> **Boy:** I do.
>
> **Socrates:** And you know that a square figure has these four lines equal?
>
> **Boy:** Certainly.
>
> **Socrates:** And these lines which I have drawn through the middle of the square are also equal?
>
> **Boy:** Certainly.
>
> Socrates continues to ask the boy questions, drawing diagrams on the board as he does so.
>
> "Do you observe, Meno," he says, "that I am not teaching the boy anything, but only asking him questions?"
>
> And Socrates goes on with his questions.
>
> "And how many spaces are there in this section?"
>
> **Boy:** Four.
>
> **Socrates:** And how many in this?
>
> **Boy:** Two.
>
> **Socrates:** And four is how many times two?
>
> **Boy:** Twice.
>
> **Socrates:** And this space is of how many feet?
>
> **Boy:** Of eight feet.
>
> **Socrates:** And from what line do you get this figure?

Boy: From this.

And presently Socrates is saying:

"And that is the line which the learned call the diagonal. And if this is the proper name, then you, Meno's slave, are prepared to affirm that the double space is the square of the diagonal?"

Boy: Certainly, Socrates.

"Well," says Socrates to Meno, "what do you say to that? I didn't tell him that! I just asked questions. He must have known it already. It was in him!—all that knowledge."

In the same way there is much, much in all of us, but we do not know it. No one ever calls it out of us, unless we are lucky enough to know very intelligent, imaginative, sympathetic people who love us and have the magnanimity to encourage us, to believe in us, by listening, by praise, by appreciation, by laughing. (Everyone knows how people who laugh easily create us by their laughter,—making us think of funnier and funnier things.)

If you are going to write you must become aware of this richness in you and come to believe in it and know it is there so that you can write opulently and with self-trust. If you once become aware of it, have faith in it, you will be all right. But it is like this: if you have a million dollars in the bank and don't know it, it doesn't do you any good.

I have sometimes collaborated with people who were not writers.[73] To help me they would write out their material, their memories of presidents, generals and so on. But it was usually very bleak and thin,—like this: "The great statesman's wife, Mrs. K.,

---

73. Incidentally the better-educated these non-writers were, the worse they wrote. The simple, uneducated people would always get some immediacy, some poetry, their true raw thoughts into their written accounts.

was a splendid hostess and entertained lavishly all the interesting personages who were in Washington that year." So my collaborator would write it down.

"How did she look? What was she like?" I would ask.

My collaborator's face would at once brighten with intelligent, excited, witty interest and she would volubly and eagerly pour out:

"She was violent, fascinating. She'd explode at a second's boredom. She had arched black eyebrows and a red face, because of high blood pressure. She walked in a rubber union suit to keep her weight down. She was generous and not a snob at all, but she couldn't stand stupidity. She'd burst like a boiler. Her husband used to hang back and turn off all the electric lights. 'That's right, Eddie,' she'd call over her shoulder. 'Turn them all out. That's right, you might save a couple of cents.' He was afraid of her and did not like to be at home."

You see how well she could have written if she had put that down.

Here is another reason why your bright imagination does not escape out of you onto paper when you write: Say that you have an article to write. You think you must begin at the beginning: "The lumber industry in the state of Minnesota"—or whatever your article is about—and then in a straight, orderly line of neat, grammatical sentences go through to the end.

Well, at once you are blocked. This seems such a frightful task confronting you,—to get this mass of material—amorphous and confused—into a thin line of sentences. And worrying about the *whole* piece, you are terribly bored and weighed down by the effort ahead, by the confusion. And so you write, moving along in slow agony and ennui. And inevitably you lose and discard all in your thoughts that is bright, ardent, true, that has variety and richness, as you painstakingly put down instead a line of drab prose.

Instead of working that way, here is something you might try:

I was in my sister's house in New York and her fourteen-year-old girl was hard pressed by parties and school work. What worried her most was a theme that had to be written. It was to be about Thoreau. It seems that Robert Louis Stevenson had written that Thoreau, because he avoided "the bracing contact with the world... was a skulker." In the theme the children were to say whether they agreed with Stevenson or not. Carlotta was a passionate admirer of Thoreau. It made her very mad to have Stevenson say that and so I knew, since she had some passion, some violence in her about it, that she could write a fine, sparkling theme. I said to her:

"Come upstairs with me and we will get your theme written in twenty minutes, and you will get an Excellent on it."

Here is what I wrote, typed rapidly, on yellow scratch paper. I put down every single word that she said even to groans and "oh, hecks."

* * *

R. L. Stevenson said: "For there is apt to be something... unmanly, something almost dastardly in a life that does not move with dash and freedom, and that fears the bracing contact of the world. In one word, Thoreau was a skulker."

Me: Well, who was he anyway? Why do you like him?

Carlotta: Let me see, who was he? I like him because I think he was being original and did what he liked, and he had the gumption to do it in spite of what everyone else was telling him and he was not dragged down by the conventional thing. I think this business of everybody jumping over the fence Oh like a lot of sheep is sort of useless and silly.

Why?

Carlotta: Well, because I think that just because everybody else thinks so it does not need to be the right thing.

How do you mean?

Carlotta: I mean I think the sheep are the cowardly ones and the odd ones really amount to something and ought to be admired. Look at history.

What in history? What do you mean?

Carlotta: Well, Andrew Jackson was greater than Grant certainly, because he followed his own opinions while Grant was trying to please others, all the time.

Where did Thoreau live?

Carlotta: Walden. We've just been studying about it. That is where he went to live in the woods and built a little house and subsisted on practically nothing, very little money, managed to keep alive, and Oh, gosh, let's see... well, he was very practical.

How do you mean?

Carlotta: He built his own house and got his own food and ate very simply and did very little work, just enough work so that he could get enough money to live on. Well, he did just exactly what he liked. He worked about six months of the year on and off, at what he liked doing.

What was it?

Carlotta: Surveying. The rest of the time he was just taking walks and studying nature.

But "studying?" That sounds like work.

Carlotta: Oh, he did it just for enjoyment, absolutely, not for the good of mankind. He didn't care a whoop about what anybody else thought or wanted. In fact, he rather enjoyed shocking everybody. In Concord he'd walk by when everybody else was in church, just to show everybody he wasn't doing anything and didn't care what they thought.

Do you think he liked people?

Carlotta: Well, I think he liked animals better. I don't think he hated people, he was just plain independent. He didn't think it was necessary to help everybody else. He thought there was enough of that going on without him.

How do you suppose he looked?

Carlotta: A handsome man I think.

Was he married?

Carlotta: Never married, no responsibility at all... didn't want any...

What about his concern about things like slavery? Did he give a whoop about that?

Carlotta: Yes, he did. He thought it was wrong, but he wasn't going to great lengths to correct it.

Was he good to animals?

Carlotta: Yes, terribly good, extraordinary. If a dog or a pig got lost he would spend days trying to get it back to his owner to be sure it wouldn't starve.

Did he ever take in a child?

Carlotta: Well, I think he would have, if there had been one. In fact, his idea was, his philosophy, that everybody should take care of themselves, that was just exactly the whole point.

How did he live?

Carlotta: He slept outdoors while building his house and then he slept inside, nice and comfortable, nothing luxurious, just a good bed and nothing more.

New Englander?

Carlotta: Yah, I think so.

The other day your father was going to the country and 1 heard you talking to your mother about Thoreau. What was that? 'What were you saying?

Carlotta: Well, Pa wanted to go to the country for the week-end and I thought I should go with him because he would like it better. But I wanted to stay in town and go to the movies. Mother said I had to decide and I said "Well, I know what Thoreau would have done... He would have gone to the movies."

But Thoreau was so crazy about the country, I thought?

Carlotta: I know. But he would have done what was right for *him*. What he really *wanted* to do, see? Not to please his relations or his surroundings, but *himself*... I thought Thoreau would have gone to the movies and so I did.

Now get back to what Stevenson said about him. What does "manly" mean?

Carlotta: Yes, all right. What does "manly" mean, what does "dastardly"? It means cowardly, yes. So Stevenson calls him a coward. But he couldn't have been, because he did have the strength to do what he thought the best. The fact is that the balance of cowardliness is with all the others; for in the world, look around and see that everybody is doing what everybody else wants to do, all the time.

What about unselfishness?

Carlotta: Well, what good does it do? if you are always wanting to do what everybody else wants you to do? If you are cross and bored by it?... Unselfishness is a very different proposition.

What is it?

Carlotta: Well...

But we had better stick to Thoreau. This matter of independence and doing what others disapprove of...

Carlotta: Well, I myself have never done anything with everybody against me. Maybe I have but I can't remember. But I would like to! The most cowardly person we know—look around and you can see, is always the one who is always trying to please everybody and uneasy if there is a single person even disapproving of their slightest actions.

I think you are right. Now let's see: Stevenson says, "a life that does not move with dash and freedom."

Carlotta: But it seems to me that is just what Thoreau did, he was so very free and dashing. He always followed his impulses, so carefree; so this man doesn't know what he is talking about, when he says "a life that does not move with dash and freedom."

What about this? "And that fears the bracing contact of the world?"

Carlotta: The point is that his life at Walden was just sort of an experiment and he had tried the world business, a great deal of it.

Where had he worked?

Carlotta: Well, he had worked for his parents. His parents ran a pencil factory. And every once in a while when the pencil factory ran down he went to work and worked the business up, and ran it for his family so it was good enough so that they could run it themselves. Well, he was just as well fitted for a successful, a so-called successful life, as any man; he was practical and smart. It wasn't a flight at all; it was a decision that what he liked best was the right thing to do and he did it.

He didn't seem to be afraid of loneliness. What do you think about that?

Carlotta: Say, that's a good ideal Yah, we'll put that in. Because what most people are most afraid of, of all, is loneliness. Take the girls I know or anybody,—they've got to crowd in and huddle wherever there is a warm, friendly bunch. Why, that is the most terrible thing of all for most people,—being alone for any length of time... So he certainly was not a skulker at all, but a brave man who was just determined to do what he felt was right. He wasn't a slave to anybody else... I guess that's all... Say I forgot something he did—write, when he was out of the woods.

What did he write?

Carlotta: Well, he wrote several books, not very important books. But he was writing. It isn't as if he was doing absolutely no work at all... He ate very unhealthy food, but it never bothered him.

What food?

Carlotta: Well, lots of bread but very little else. He said he never found any need for any meat or an expensive supply of vegetables... Heck, that's enough. That's enough for anyone.

* * *

Carlotta took the five typewritten pages I had written,—her own words. She cut and pasted and re-arranged them somewhat. For vague, inexact words, she substituted here and there better and more discriminating ones. Where a thought was dim and clumsily uttered, it was easy on second writing to see it clearly and to tell more about it. But a surprising number of her original sentences were right. The involuntary utterance had gone straight to the point, and could not be improved.

This re-writing of her first draft was the work of an hour. And it was pleasurable and absorbing work, not a brain-addling labor.

And what she wrote about Thoreau had life and was interesting because she said just exactly what she thought, though I helped to pull it out of her by questions. On the theme she got an "Excellent."

And so try this yourself when you write an article. Do not worry about the whole. Write what is next, the idea that comes now at the moment. Don't be afraid. For there will be more coherence and arrangement in your thoughts than you think.

And one more thing. Who knows if he is great or talented? No one. We don't even know what we are, or what our lives are like.

A woman I know sat in a quiet room in her house every day and looked out at the frozen lake and thoughtfully put down what she thought and what was happening day after day—what her little girl said, her husband, the small events of their lives together.

She typewrote this out on yellow sheets of paper and put them away—a big, accumulating pile in a drawer and did not read them again-for nearly a year. The queer thing was that as she sat there writing and looking at the lake she thought of herself as a pleasant, middle-aged woman with a quiet, ordinary, comfortable, rather uninteresting life.

But a year later when she looked at what she had written—when it had become cold and separate from her, like the writing of a stranger—she was utterly astounded. In the first place she could hardly believe it because it was so good!

"Why, it is very good,—startling, remarkable!" she wrote to me. "You know it could be made into a novel and I would call it 'One Year' but it would be my whole life; my whole existence is epitomized in it. And I find that instead of having a quiet, pleasant, ordinary life, I have the most violent, extraordinary, terrific life... And the picture of my little girl stands out like a painting by Goya."

You see, what she wrote was more true of her than her own idea of herself. *I* knew what an impassioned, wonderful person she was, though she could never be aware of it herself.

Van Gogh wrote:

"Who will be in figure painting what Claude Monet is in landscape... I would be heartily glad if a kind of Guy de Maupassant in painting came along to paint light-heartedly the beautiful people and things here... But this painter who is to come—I can't imagine him living in little cafes working away with false teeth as I do."

Chekhov did not know that he was a great writer. Or I should put it this way: Van Gogh and Chekhov and all great people have known inwardly that they were something. They have had a passionate conviction of their importance, of the life, the fire, the god in them. But they were never sure that *others* would necessarily see it in them, or that recognition would ever come.

But this is the point: everybody in the world has the same conviction of inner importance, fire, of the god within. The tragedy is that either they stifle their fire by not believing in it and using it; or they try to prove to the world and themselves that they have it, not inwardly and greatly, but externally and egotistically, by some second-rate thing like money or power or more publicity.

Therefore all should work. First because it is impossible that you have *no* creative gift. Second: the only way to make it live and increase is to use it. Third: you cannot be sure that it is not a *great* gift.

And so I think Blake's attitude toward his genius is the right one. We should all feel as he did. He knew about his inner fire and believed in it. "He knows himself greatly who never opposes his genius." He never hindered or discouraged it or let anyone else do so. He cast out all prudence: "Prudence is a rich, ugly, old maid courted by incapacity," he said. Moderation, caution, measuring, weighing and comparing—"I will not Reason & Compare," he said; "my business is to Create!"

He abhorred that conceit and cowardice that thinks it is modesty.[74]

The fox, the mole, the beetle and the bat
By sweet reserve and modesty get fat.

Blake wrote and drew and painted what his Vision and Imagination showed to him with enthusiasm and joy. Much of it he burned and threw away carelessly for he said that earthly fame just detracted from spiritual glory. He knew that in spite of the neglect of his time that his work was great and important, for the Eternal Powers do not labor in vain.

My designs unchanged remain,
Time may rage but rage in vain.
High above Time's troubled fountains,
On the great Atlantic mountains,
In my golden house on high,
There they shine eternally.

That is what I urge all of you, and myself, to do: work and shine eternally.

74. It is just fear of acting and making mistakes. It is a refusal to follow one's vision. It is a wish to get everybody's approval by being utterly harmless, a zero.

16

On Using the Imagination

I want to say something about using the imagination. Everybody has it, though not believing in it enough. People when they write, try too hard, try to force it.

For years I persuaded myself it was hard to use the imagination. Not so. The only hard part in using it is the anxiety, the fear of being mediocre. For example, I would think: "Now I will write a story," and sit down expecting to swim into it, and begin: "John Johnson was a..." and strike a snag because I realized I didn't know yet how he looked or what he was, and then came discouragement at once and dreadful fear that I was a person without imagination.

If it were not for that fear, one would press on all day, quietly trying to see John Johnson, with as much pleasure as weeding a garden, until one had a clear picture of him at last.

But now I know that imagination comes, works, when you are *not* trying, when you have a peculiar passive clarity. A friend of mine has frequently the same dream. In it a procession of people begin coming, all strange and unknown, with fascinating faces and costumes, and she thinks in her dream when she sees the procession coming: "Oh, good! here they come!" as though it were a parade for her own delectation. She makes no effort, just deliciously relaxes. And I think it is something like this that characters in your story or your novel come before you and show themselves.

And I think this too because of what a friend of mine, a young Swedish mystic and clairvoyant, tells me. She sees visions just as Blake did: saints, archangels, heroes. She shuts her eyes and these radiant beings appear before her, much more clearly and minutely than she could see something with her "mortal and perishing eye," as Blake put it,[75] and she tells just how they look and what they say. I cannot explain what she sees or *why* she sees, but I know that if I could see as she does, with that glorious, incomparable Dantesque imagination, I would be blessed beyond belief.

I have asked her a thousand questions about it.

She says:

> When I become practical I can't do it. For instance, I have my eyes shut and I tell what I see and someone says: "But you see only such beautiful things. There must be some bad things too." And I think: "Well, I suppose there must be." But as soon as I *try* to see, I cannot do it at all. Then it *all* goes,—all this power to see "across."

This is how Mozart composed,—that inexhaustible, free fountain of incredibly beautiful music. These are his words:

I really can say no more on this subject than the following: for I myself know no more about it and cannot account for it. When I am, as it were, *completely myself*, entirely alone, and of good cheer—say traveling in a carriage, or walking after a good meal, or during the night when I cannot sleep; it is on such occasions that my ideas flow best and most abundantly. Whence and how they come I know not; nor can I force them. Those ideas that please me, I retain in memory and am accustomed, as I have been told, to

75. He called this vision—seeing eye "the immortal and imaginative organ."

hum them to myself. If I continue in this way it soon occurs to me how I may turn this or that morsel to account so as to make a good dish of it, that is to say, agreeable to the rules of counterpoint, to the peculiarities of the various instruments.

All this fires my soul, and provided I am not disturbed, my subject enlarges itself, becomes methodized and defined, and the whole, though it be long, stands almost complete and finished in my mind, so that I can survey it, like a fine picture, a beautiful statue, at a glance. Nor do I hear in my imagination the parts successively, but I hear them as it were, gleich alles zusammen, all at once. What a delight that is I cannot tell! All this inventing, this producing, takes place in a pleasing, lively dream. Still the actual hearing of the tout ensemble, is after all the best. What has been produced I do not easily forget, and this is perhaps the best gift I have my Divine Maker to thank for.

We cannot be all like Mozart. But we are all something like him. I don't think we trust our imaginations enough, use them rightly. Self-trust is so important. When you launch on a story, make your neck loose, feel free, good-natured. And be lazy. Feel that you are going to throw it away. Try writing utterly unplanned stories and see what comes out.

Sometimes I would give my class a brief plot, just the barest skeleton, and tell them to sit down and write it off in this self-trusting way. "Feel as you do when you are telling children a great, big lie and making it up as you go along—pulling their legs with a whopper."

The results were just astonishing. One gentle, aristocratic woman in a few minutes had written a story and had drawn such a good portrait of a chorus girl that she was almost shocked at what she had done. She had drawn also the portrait of a sanctimonious business man with a passion for genealogy, who was being discreetly unfaithful to his wife. The gentle, aristocratic lady had never known a chorus girl, perhaps never seen one. Nor had she ever known such an obnoxious business man. There they were, though, these two people, created in no time with true, deft lines.

Try this. You will then learn about the powers that are in you, all the endless stories not only from this life but from all your former incarnations.

Here is another suggestion that might help you:

I have said that art is a generosity, i.e., you tell somebody something not to show off but because you want to share it with them.

Once I was playing the piano and a musician, overhearing it, said to me: "It isn't *going* anywhere. You must always play to *someone*—it may be to the river, or God, or to someone who is dead, or to someone in the room, but it must go somewhere."

That is why it helps often, to have an imaginary listener when you are writing, telling a story, so that you will be interesting and convincing throughout. You know how a listener helps to shape and create the story. Say that you are telling a story to children. You instinctively tell it, change it, adapt it, cut it, expand it, all under their large, listening eyes, so that they will be arrested and held by it throughout.

Do that when writing. You have to hold your audience in writing to the very end—much more than in talking, when people have to be polite and listen to you.

This recognition that art, music, literature is a sharing, that a live, alternating current is passing swiftly between teller and listener, that a listener (even though imaginary or transcendent) is absolutely essential in the process, cleared up many things that puzzled me.

For instance this Art for Art's sake business. I used to try to write something that was governed by that maxim. Yes, I tackled sometimes an attempt at pure, unadulterated Art wherein I would be utterly scornful and haughty toward all outsiders, snobbishly disregarding all readers, indifferent as to whether anyone liked it at all—but myself. Well, why was it so dull then? so utterly disgustingly bad? this "pure Art" I turned out?

Certainly one reason was that I had not that friendly, generous humbleness to want to interest, entertain or make clear to others what I thought. It just became a literary stunt—though this kind of literature and art is often admired by people of the very highest brow.

But when you come to think of it, the Iliad, the psalms, the sagas, all the great literature of old, were creatively affected and molded by the fact that there were listeners. Imagine Homer or Dante, the minstrels, the bards, the saga-tellers, standing up before their audiences and smiting the lyre and then (utterly ungenerous and indifferent as to whether anyone would be interested or not, very contemptuous in fact of this "listening" which is an electric current that anyone can feel and that brings the narrator to life) just revealing their psychology.

I think this is the trouble with subjective writing: no generosity, no living current exchanged with a listener.

Chekhov wrote to his brother, advising him about his writing:

> There is a story of yours where a young couple sit kissing each other all through the dinner, and talking rubbish. There's not a single sensible word, but thorough *complacency. And you are not writing for the reader.* You wrote because that chatter pleased *you*... Subjectivity is an awful thing—even for the reason that it betrays the poor writer hand over fist. Why don't you describe the dinner—how they ate, what they ate, what the cook was like, how vulgar your hero was, how satisfied with his lazy contentment, how ridiculous the heroine's love for that smug, napkinned, overfed gander?... You know so well how to laugh, to bite, to sneer; you have such a well-rounded style.

All this is why you cannot (I have found from experience) write a long, long book, four-fifths full of your own psychological writhings, your own entrails all pinned out on the surgical table. Who cares? Besides, because of the Third Dimension, every reader knows at once that you are a snob and an egotist and do not care about anyone but yourself. So the reader flags and thinks with a feeling of exhaustion: "Why read more? He isn't going to tell me anything. He is talking to himself."

17

The Tigers of Wrath are Wiser than the Horses of Instruction

William Blake

A practical friend of mine, a careful planner, said to me when I told him this book (which I have thought about for so long) must be written and finished by a certain time:

"Have you planned the book? Have you got your outline firmly in mind?" and thereby made a coldness come around my heart and I suffered several minutes of panic, the most intense anxiety.

But I said:

"*No!* Of course I haven't planned it. I wouldn't think of planning it."

For when you begin to plan such a huge edifice of words, your heart fails you. It is too hard, it will never get done, it is too complex and frightful. No, write what comes to you now. More will come later. The river will begin to flow through you.

It took me years to learn this. Until recently I would have followed what they all advised and planned it, written out a concise, logical outline—Roman numerals I and II with sub-titles a, b and c. And nobody would read the book because it would not only be frightfully dull but not true, because throughout I would be forcing things and bits of things into the splendid logical and sterile outline. "Wouldn't this little quotation from Confucius be rather nice in it? Perhaps I could just slip it in under the chapter entitled: 'Constructive thinking, or Things the new writer must be careful to avoid.' Or perhaps I could squeeze it in this chapter on 'How to Construct a Plot.'"

No, I wouldn't think of planning the book before I write it. You write, and plan it afterwards. You write it first because every word must come out with freedom, and with meaning because you think it is so and want to tell it. If this is done the book will be alive. I don't mean that it will be successful. It may be alive to only ten people. But to those ten at least it will be alive. It will speak to them. It will help to free them.

That is why I think English teachers and all short story courses put the cart before the horse. (So they do in art schools too, I hear.) In English courses, you study plot-construction and sharpen your anxious brows as the tailor does on the needle's eye, over all these necessities, before you begin your story. But you should tell the story first. Everybody can tell a story. If you have ever told a story to a child so that he would listen, you can tell a story.

That is why I don't like critics, whether they are English professors, or friends, or members of one's family, or men of letters on literary reviews. It is so easy for them to annihilate us, first by discouragement[76] and then by shackling our imagination in rules so that we cannot work freely and well on the next thing.

Nobody knows better than I how sensitive writers are. But it is inevitable. It is nothing to be ashamed of. Since our wish to create something is the life of the Spirit, I think that when people condemn what we do, they are symbolically destroying us.

---

76. Remember that discouragement is the only illness, George Bernard Shaw says.

Hence the excruciatingly painful feeling, though to our common sense it seems foolish and self-centered to feel so badly.

In my diary I find this about my class:

"It is interesting how if inside, my interest in anyone of them flags, they know it; or if I allow discouragement to creep into any of them for one minute, they die away. Tender plants. So must read from *all* their manuscripts."

If I just read from *some* of the manuscripts the others would think: "She is good. I am no good," and begin to despair.

I wish I could show you why I object to critics and why I think they do harm and stifle and obstruct all creative power. It was William Blake who revealed this to me.

"What we so often call Reason," Blake said, "is not the Understanding at all but is merely derived from the experience of our five senses, derived from Earth and from our bodies."

"You cannot do this," Reason says (and all those erudite critics) "because it did not work the last time. Besides, it was logically and scientifically established by so-and-so after plenty of experiments," says the rationalist, the materialistic scientist, the critic, basing all this on merely physical experiences and so shutting out the glories of their Vision, their Imagination, which is Divine and comes from God and cannot be weighed and measured by scientists, established and explained. This Vision might tell them something new, miraculous and great if they would only let it. But their hard-shell of skeptical intellectuality keeps it out.

Blake said:

"All that is Valuable in Knowledge is *Superior* to Demonstrative Science, such as is Weighed and Measured," and he says, "Reason, or All we have known, is not the same it shall be when we know More."

And how will we know more? Only through the Imagination which comes from God, which the prophets and all great people have spoken.[77]

Blake abhorred Francis Bacon and the eighteenth century rationalists that followed him.

"I have read Locke, Bacon, Burke. On Everyone of these books I wrote my opinion, and on looking them over find that I felt the same contempt and abhorrence then that I do now... They mock inspiration and vision. Inspiration and Vision was then, and now is, and I hope will always be, my element, my eternal dwelling place; how can I then hear it Contemned without returning Scorn for Scorn?"

Blake saw visions, the arch-angel Gabriel and other great beings who told him what to write and draw and how to invent a new method of engraving. "The divine Blake," said his friend Calvert, "who had seen God, sir, and had talked with angels."

Blake of course thought the Imagination and inspiration (which we all have, as I have said) came from God and through God's messengers. The psychologists tell us it is from the unconscious. But one explanation is as good as another. I like Blake's better because it is much easier to understand, more plausible.

But to get back to the critics, who obstruct and frighten imagination away, in themselves and others. It is plain from the history of architecture, painting and sculpture, that men begin to theorize critically only when inspiration has died down. But inspiration only dies down because the theoreticians, the horses of instruction, begin to dissect, analyze and then codify into rules what yesterday's great artists did freely from their true selves.

Another reason I don't like critics (the one in myself as well as in other people) is that they try to teach something without *being* it. They are like all those feeble, knock-kneed women afraid of

---

77. There have been great imaginative scientists too, of course.

bugs and burglars, who say to their husbands (in so many words): "Go out and fight, you coward!" They are second-raters who have not the courage or love to make anything themselves. Or they are like big game hunters, killing from a great, safe distance, with great ego-satisfaction (though they are entirely safe themselves and the shooting requires no muscular effort and not much skill) some nice little creature.

Of course I am sorry for them too. Because by encouraging the critic in themselves (the hater) they have killed the artist (the lover). Know that if you have a kind of cultured know-it-all in yourself who takes pleasure in pointing out what is not good, in discriminating, reasoning and comparing, you are bound under a knave. I wish you could be delivered.

For I know that the energy of the creative impulse comes from love and all its manifestations—admiration, compassion, glowing respect, gratitude, praise, compassion, tenderness, adoration, enthusiasm.

Compare the tenderness of great artists with the attitude of critics towards other men.

"You are kind to painters," Van Gogh wrote to his brother, "and I tell you the more I think, the more I feel that there is nothing more truly artistic than to love people."

And when this brother said a certain artist was "mediocre," Van Gogh could not bear it. "That quite depends on what you call mediocre," he wrote. "Mediocre in its simple signification I do not despise at all. And one certainly does not rise above that mark by despising what is mediocre. In my opinion one must begin by at least having some respect for the mediocre and know that it already means something, and that it is only reached through great difficulty. Adieu for the present, I shake hands with you in thought."

When Sir Joshua Reynolds wrote: "Enthusiastic admiration seldom promotes knowledge," Blake wrote furiously in the margin of the book: "Enthusiastic admiration is the First Principle of

Knowledge and its last. Now he begins to degrade, to Deny and to Mock."

And remember the word "enthusiasm" means "divine inspiration."

I read in *Harper's Magazine* a few years ago an article by a highly educated man wherein he told with what conscientious pains he had brought up all his children to be skeptical of everything, never to believe anything in life or religion or their own feelings without submitting it to many rational doubts, to have a persistent, thoroughly skeptical, doubting attitude toward everything. In other words to weazen and kill in themselves all spontaneous love, passion, enthusiasm, all creative power. I think he might as well have taken them out in the backyard and killed them with an ax.

And so in your own work, whatever you love will be easy to write or paint. One day many of us went painting[78] in the country. The others looked for sections in the landscape that would make "interesting compositions." "Mine will be the best," I told them. Because I looked for something to paint that I *liked*, something that I felt a fierce, delighted enthusiasm for—two carriages with spidery red and yellow wheels flashing highlights in the sunshine. And my painting was best. Not because I had more skill or talent than the others, but because I liked what I looked at, was filled with a vehement energy over it.

It is because of the critics, the doubters (in the outer world and within ourselves) that we have such hesitancy when we write. And I know the hesitancy just mars it. It does not make it better at all.

As I write this I many times have had the chilling feeling come around my heart because of the thought: "What if it may not be true? People will say I am crazy. Where is my logic? I haven't a Ph.D. in philosophy or psychology."

---

78. Most of us had never painted before. A few had done it a little bit.

But I don't let the cold feeling stay there because, just the same, I know what I say is true, because it is true to me and therefore I say it freely and you must have it. A few years ago I would not have dared say anything in this book without looking up long, corroborating passages in big books: "William James says," etc., etc.

I believe now in speaking from myself, as I want you to do when you write. Don't keep marshaling thoughts like: "I must prove it."

You don't *have* to prove it[79] by citing scientific examples, by comparing and all. Say it. If it is true to you, it is true. Another truth may take its place later. What comes truly from me is true, whether anybody believes it or not. It is *my* truth.

Therefore when you write, speak with complete self-trust and do not timidly qualify and feel the ice of well authenticated literary usage and critical soundness—so afraid when you have finished writing that they will riddle you full of holes.

Let them. Later if you find what you wrote isn't true, accept the new truth. Consistency is the horror of the world.

---

79. Unless you want to, of course; unless that is the purpose of what you are writing.

18

He whose Face Gives No Light shall Never Become a Star

Blake

Why urge everybody to write when the world 1s so full of writers, and there are oceans of printed matter?

Well, all of it does not amount to very much and little is worth remembering. Every two or three years a book comes out and everyone likes it very much and praises it and says it is a true work of art. And for these books I am grateful. But there could be a great deal more living literature, that really talks to people and does not just kill time for them.

And what is a little book or two, when there is so much greatness in the world hidden all around us? These good things that appear in print seem so meager, so slight, so publisher-touted, in this country of a hundred million people. Now one or two little books—making an impression for two years, forgotten utterly in five—that is not enough, when you think what there might be, what might come out of people.

But if (as I wish) everybody writes and respects and loves writing, then we would have a nation of intelligent, eager, impassioned readers; and generous and grateful ones, not mere critical, logy, sedentary passengers, *observers* of writing, whose attitude is: "All right: entertain me now." Then we would all talk to each other in our writing with excitement and passionate interest, like free men and brothers, and like the people in paradise, whom Dostoevsky described in a story: "not only in their songs but in all their lives they seemed to do nothing but admire each other." The result: some great, great national literature.

And this is all that I have to say.

To sum up—if you want to write:

1. Know that you have talent, are original and have something important to say.

2. Know that it is good to work. Work with love and think of liking it when you do it. It is easy and interesting. It is a privilege. There is nothing hard about it but your anxious vanity and fear of failure.

3. Write freely, recklessly, in first drafts.

4. Tackle anything you want to—novels, plays, anything. Only remember Blake's admonition: "Better to strangle an infant in its cradle than nurse unacted desires."

5. Don't be afraid of writing bad stories. To discover what is wrong with a story write two new ones and then go back to it.

6. Don't fret or be ashamed of what you have written in the past. How I always suffered from this! How I would regurgitate out of my memory (and still do) some nauseous little lumps of things I had written! But don't do this. Go on to the next. And fight against this tendency which is much of it due not to splendid modesty, but a

lack of self-respect. We are too ready (women especially) not to stand by what we have said or done. Often it is a way of forestalling criticism, saying hurriedly: "I know it is awful!" before anyone else does. Very bad and cowardly. It is so conceited and timid to be ashamed of one's mistakes. Of *course* they are mistakes. Go on to the next.

7. Try to discover your true, honest, untheoretical self.

8. Don't think of yourself as an intestinal tract and tangle of nerves in the skull, that will not work unless you drink coffee. Think of yourself as incandescent power, illuminated perhaps and forever talked to by God and his messengers. Remember how wonderful you are, what a miracle! Think if Tiffany's made a mosquito, how wonderful we would think it was!

9. If you are never satisfied with what you write, that is a good sign. It means your vision can see so far that it is hard to come up to it. Again I say, the only unfortunate people are the glib ones, immediately satisfied with their work. To them the ocean is only knee-deep.

10. When discouraged, remember what Van Gogh said: "If you hear a voice within you saying: You are no painter, then paint by all means, lad, and that voice will be silenced, but only by working."

11. Don't be afraid of yourself when you write. Don't check-rein yourself. If you are afraid of being sentimental, say, for heaven's sake be as sentimental as you can or feel like being! Then you will probably pass through to the other side and slough off sentimentality because you understand it at last and really don't care about it.

12. Don't always be appraising yourself, wondering if you are better or worse than other writers. "I will not Reason & Compare," said Blake; "my business is to Create."

Besides, since you are like no other being ever created since the beginning of Time, you are incomparable.

And why should you do all these things? Why should we all use our creative power and write or paint or play music, or whatever it tells us to do?

Because there is nothing that makes people so generous, joyful, lively, bold and compassionate, so indifferent to fighting and the accumulation of objects and money. Because the best way to know the Truth or Beauty is to try to express it. And what is the purpose of existence Here or Yonder but to discover truth and beauty and express it, i.e., share it with others?

And so I really believe this book will hasten the Millennium by two or three hundred years. And if it has given you the impulse to write one small story, then I am pleased.

INTERNATIONAL BESTSELLER

THE POWER OF YOUR

SUBCONSCIOUS MIND

by Dr. Joseph Murphy

Price	:	Rs. 195
Pages	:	232
Size	:	7.75x5.25 inches
Binding	:	Paperback
Language	:	English
Subject	:	Self-Help
ISBN	:	9788180320958

'The Power of Your Subconscious Mind' has been a bestseller since its first publication in 1963, selling many millions of copies since its original publication. It is one of the most brilliant and beloved spiritual self-help works of all time which can help you heal yourself, banish your fears, sleep better, enjoy better relationships and just feel happier. The techniques are simple and results come quickly. You can improve your relationships, your finances, your physical well-being.

Dr Joseph Murphy explains that life events are actually the result of the workings of your conscious and subconscious minds. He suggests practical techniques through which one can change one's destiny, principally by focusing and redirecting this miraculous energy. Years of research studying the world's major religions convinced him that some Great Power lay behind all spiritual life and that this power is within each of us.

'The Power of Your Subconscious Mind' will open a world of success, happiness, prosperity, and peace for you.

OTHER BOOKS YOU MAY LIKE

- A Christmas Carol by Charles Dickens, ISBN: 9788193545874
- Anthem by Ayn Rand, ISBN: 9789389157079
- Apni Chhamta Pehchaniye by NK Sondhi, ISBN: 9788193545843
- As a Man Thinketh by James Allen, ISBN: 9788180320262
- Awakened Imagination by Neville Goddard, ISBN: 9789389157086
- Be What You Wish by Neville Goddard, ISBN: 9789387669550
- Becoming a Writer by Dorothea Brande, ISBN: 9789389157093
- Believe in Yourself by Joseph Murphy, ISBN: 9789388118385
- Civilization and Its Discontents by Sigmund Freud, ISBN: 9789387669499
- Feeling is the Secret by Neville Goddard, ISBN: 9789389157109
- Gita According to Gandhi by Mahatma Gandhi, ISBN: 9788180320040
- Gravity by George Gamow, ISBN: 9789388118484
- Great Speeches of Abraham Lincoln by Abraham Lincoln, ISBN: 9789380914336
- How to Attract Money by Joseph Murphy, ISBN: 9789388118408
- How to be filled with the Holy Spirit by A. W. Tozer, ISBN: 9789389157116
- How to Dev Self Conf and Imp Pub Speaking by Carnegie, ISBN: 9789387669000
- How to Enjoy Your Life and Your Job by Dale Carnegie, ISBN: 9789387669017
- How to Stop Worrying and Start Living by Dale Carnegie, ISBN: 9789380914817
- Julius Caesar by William Shakespeare, ISBN: 9789380914374
- Macbeth by William Shakespeare, ISBN: 9789380914343
- Madhubala by Manju Gupta, ISBN: 9789380914961
- Meditations by Marcus Aurelius, ISBN: 9789388118736
- Mein Kampf (My Struggle) by Adolf Hitler, ISBN: 9789380914855
- Metamorphosis by Franz Kafka, ISBN: 9788180320057
- Mother by Maxim Gorky, ISBN: 9788180320330
- My Experiments with Truth by Mahatma Gandhi, ISBN: 9789387669291

OTHER BOOKS YOU MAY LIKE

- My Inventions: The Autobiography of Tesla by Nikola Tesla, ISBN: 9789388118132
- My Life : Albert Einstein by GP Editors, ISBN: 9789388118941
- My Life : Dilip Kumar by GP Editors, ISBN: 9789388118934
- Quiz For All by Dr. Ruth Premi, ISBN: 9788180320897
- Romeo and Juliet by William Shakespeare, ISBN: 9789380914329
- Save Your Child by NK Sondhi, ISBN: 9789388118361
- Selected Short Stories of James Joyce by James Joyce, ISBN: 9788180320392
- Selected Stories of Rabindranath Tagore by Rab Tagore, ISBN: 9789380914770
- Sense and Sensibility by Jane Austen, ISBN: 9789380914589
- Tales from Shakespeare by Charles Lamb, Mary Lamb, ISBN: 9789380914367
- The Alchemy of Happiness by Al-Ghazzali, ISBN: 9789387669505
- The Art of Public Speaking by Dale Carnegie, ISBN: 9788180320422
- The Art of War by Sun Tzu, ISBN: 9789380914893
- The Autobiography of a Yogi by Paramahansa Yogananda, ISBN: 9789380914602
- The Autobiography of Benjamin Franklin by Ben Franklin, ISBN: 9788190276689
- The Bhagavad Gita by Sir Edwin Arnold, ISBN: 9789380914275
- The Canterville Ghost by Oscar Wilde, ISBN: 9789380914527
- The Dynamic Laws of Prosperity by Catherine Ponder, ISBN: 9789388118156
- The Game of Life and How to Play It by Florence S. Shinn, ISBN: 9789387669390
- The Great Gatsby by F. Scott Fitzgerald, ISBN: 9789380914473
- The Greatest Short Stories of Leo Tolstoy by Leo Tolstoy, ISBN: 9788180320002
- The Imitation of Christ by Thomas À Kempis, ISBN: 9789388118057
- The Invisible Man by H.G. Wells, ISBN: 9788193545850
- The Jungle Book by Rudyard Kipling, ISBN: 9788193545867
- The Knowledge of the Holy by A. W. Tozer, ISBN: 9789389157130
- The Law of Success by Napoleon Hill, ISBN: 9788180320927

Develop your reading habit | **Gift books to your friends**

OTHER BOOKS YOU MAY LIKE

- The Little Prince by Antoine De Saint-Exupéry, ISBN: 9788180320590
- The Magic of Believing by Claudie Bristol, ISBN: 9789388118149
- The Magic of Faith by Joseph Murphy, ISBN: 9789388118743
- The Miracles of Your Mind by Joseph Murphy, ISBN: 9788180320743
- The Origin of Species by Charles Darwin, ISBN: 9788180320453
- The Path of Prosperity by James Allen, ISBN: 9789387669512
- The Power of Awareness by Neville Goddard, ISBN: 9789387669406
- The Power of Concentration by Theron Q. Dumont, ISBN: 9789388118064
- The Prince by Niccolò Machiavelli, ISBN: 9789387669024
- The Prophet by Kahlil Gibran, ISBN: 9789380914022
- The Psychopathology of Everyday Life by Sigmund Freud, ISBN: 9789388118071
- The Pursuit of God by A. W. Tozer, ISBN: 9789389157147
- The Quick and Easy Way to Effe. Speaking by D. Carnegie, ISBN: 9789387669031
- The Seven Laws of Teaching by John Milton Gregory, ISBN: 9789387669413
- The Story of My Life by Helen Keller, ISBN: 9789380914541
- The Upanishads by Swami Paramananda, ISBN: 9789388118750
- The Wit and Wisdom of Gandhi by Mahatma Gandhi, ISBN: 9789380914039
- Think and Grow Rich by Napoleon Hill, ISBN: 9788180320255
- Thought Vibration by William Walker Atkinson, ISBN: 9789389157154
- Three Men in a Boat by Jerome K. Jerome, ISBN: 9789380914442
- Treasure Island by Robert Louis Stevenson, ISBN: 9788193545881
- Up From Slavery by Booker T. Washington, ISBN: 9789380914565
- Wake Up and Live! by Dorothea Brande, ISBN: 9789387669574
- Walden and Civil Disobedience by Henry David Thoreau, ISBN: 9788180320507
- Wuthering Heights by Emily Brontë, ISBN: 9788193545898
- Your Faith is Your Fortune by Neville Goddard, ISBN: 9789389157161

Develop your reading habit | Gift books to your friends